Old Age in the Welfare State

Little, Brown Series on Gerontology

Series Editors   Jon Hendricks
and
Robert Kastenbaum

Published

W. Andrew Achenbaum
Shades of Gray:
Old Age,
American Values,
and Federal Policies
Since 1920

Donald E. Gelfand
Aging: The Ethnic
Factor

Jennie Keith
Old People
As People: Social
and Cultural
Influences on
Aging and Old Age

Theodore H. Koff
Long-Term Care:
An Approach to
Serving the Frail
Elderly

Robert R. McCrae and
Paul T. Costa, Jr.
Emerging Lives,
Enduring Dispositions:
Personality in Adulthood

John Myles
Old Age in
the Welfare State:
The Political Economy
of Public Pensions

Jan D. Sinnott,
Charles S. Harris,
Marilyn R. Block,
Stephen Collesano,
and
Solomon G. Jacobson
Applied Research
in Aging: A Guide to
Methods and Resources

Martha Storandt
Counseling and
Therapy with
Older Adults

Albert J. E. Wilson III
Social Services
for Older Persons

Forthcoming
Titles

Linda M. Breytspraak
The Development
of Self in Later Life

Carroll L. Estes,
Lenore E. Gerard,
Jane Sprague Zones,
and James S. Swan
Political Economy,
Health, and Aging

Old Age in the Welfare State

The Political Economy of Public Pensions

John Myles
Carleton University
Ottawa

Little, Brown and Company
Boston   Toronto

Library of Congress Cataloging in Publication Data

Myles, John F.
  Old age in the welfare state.

  (Little Brown series on gerontology)
  Bibliography: p.
  Includes index.
  1. Old age pensions. 2. Social security. 3. Welfare
state. I. Title. II. Series.
HD7105.3.M94 1984   331.25′2   83-24923
ISBN 0-316-59367-2
ISBN 0-316-59366-4 (pbk.)

Library of Congress Catalog Card Number 83-24923

ISBN 0-316-59367-2

ISBN 0-316-59366-4 (pbk.)

9 8 7 6 5 4 3 2 1

ALP

Published simultaneously in Canada
by Little, Brown & Company (Canada) Limited

Printed in the United States of America

Foreword

Where is it? In each of the billions of cells in our bodies? Or in our minds? Then, again, perhaps it is something that happens *between* people. Ought we not also take a look at the marketplace as well? And at the values expressed through our cultural institutions? Undoubtedly, the answer lies in all these factors—and more. The phenomenon of aging takes place within our bodies, in our minds, between ourselves and others, and in culturally defined patterns.

The study and analysis of aging—a burgeoning field—is deserving of an integrated spectrum approach. Now, Little, Brown and Company offers such a perspective, one designed to respond to the diversity and complexity of the subject matter and to individualized instructional needs. The Little, Brown Series on Gerontology provides a series of succinct and readable books that encompass a wide variety of topics and concerns. Each volume, written by a highly qualified gerontologist, will provide a degree of precision and specificity not available in a general text whose coverage, expertise, and interest level cannot help but be uneven. While the scope of the gerontology series is indeed broad, individual volumes provide accurate, up-to-date presentations unmatched in the literature of gerontology.

The Little, Brown Series on Gerontology:

—provides a comprehensive overview
—explores emerging challenges and extends the frontiers of knowledge
—is organically interrelated via cross-cutting themes
—consists of individual volumes prepared by the most qualified experts

—offers maximum flexibility as teaching material

—ensures manageable length without sacrificing concepts, facts, methods, or issues

With the Little, Brown Series on Gerontology now becoming available, instructors can select the texts most desirable for their individual courses. Practitioners and other professionals will also find the foundations necessary to remain abreast of their own particular areas. No doubt, students too will respond to the knowledge and enthusiasm of gerontologists writing about only those topics they know and care most about.

Little, Brown and Company and the editors are pleased to provide a series that not only looks at conceptual and theoretical questions but squarely addresses the most critical and applied concerns of the 1980s. Knowledge without action is unacceptable. The reverse is no better.

As the list of volumes makes clear, some books focus primarily on research and theoretical concerns, others on the applied; by this two-sided approach they draw upon the most significant and dependable thinking available. It is hoped that they will serve as a wellspring for developments in years to come.

Acknowledgments

The research for this volume was made possible by a grant from the Social Science and Humanities Research Council of Canada under its strategic grants program in population aging. Much of the initial work was carried out during my stay as a visiting fellow in the Department of Sociology and the Center for European Studies at Harvard University, where I benefited from the insights of numerous colleagues. Of these, I owe particular thanks to Gösta Esping-Andersen, who not only spent many hours sharing his considerable knowledge of contemporary welfare politics with me, but also read and critically commented on the first draft of this book. Brian Gratton and Jon Hendricks also provided important detailed comments. I owe my greatest debt to my spouse and intellectual colleague, Monica Boyd, who nurtured both me and my ideas throughout the preparation of this volume. In contrast, our daughter Jennifer maintained an attitude of unwavering indifference to our discussions of old-age pensions, something I trust she will correct by the time she is 6. The book is dedicated to Monica and to my two favorite "elders," Polly and Cliff.

Contents

List of Tables

Old Age in the Welfare State

Introduction

This book arises from an observation that is at once mundane and historically startling: in all postwar capitalist democracies, economic responsibility for the maintenance of the elderly has been assumed by the state. Because retirement and receipt of a public pension at or near age 65 is now universal, state responsibility for the elderly has become a taken-for-granted part of everyday life in these countries—thus, it seems mundane. But the fact that a majority of persons over the age of 65 receive the major portion of their income from the state, irrespective of capacity to work, is both historically novel and not entirely expected in view of the principles of social organization upon which these societies were founded.

The advent of the welfare state* transformed the very character of old age in the twentieth century. Public pension systems and other social programs for the elderly made possible the spread of the retirement principle by which individuals are permitted, required, or induced to leave the labor force prior to actual physiological decline. Throughout the nineteenth century and well into the twentieth century, the majority of old people did not retire. They were more likely than the young to be out of work through unemployment or disability, but retirement per se was generally a privilege of those with independent means who had no necessity to labor in order to sustain themselves. The "elders" of the community were defined less by

---

*The term "welfare state" is used here to refer to those government policies that assign income and other consumption entitlements (including health and social services), regardless of how these entitlements are financed. Thus, welfare includes all forms of public entitlement programs including those that are "earned" by virtue of individual contributions.

1

chronological age than by institutional seniority, particularly within the family. Being old meant that one held a particular position within a system of generations—having adult children and grandchildren—rather than that one was a member of an age cohort defined by date of birth. The transformation of old age into a social category to which one gains access by virtue of reaching a specified age was made possible by the establishment of a set of age-based income entitlements administered by the state—that is, the public pension.

This turn of events in the history of old age is made even more curious by the social and political environment from which it emerged. How did it come to pass that those very societies committed to a liberal philosophy of minimal state intervention in economic affairs created for their elderly members a public system of income entitlements unprecedented in history? Why was it that the "wages" of the elderly were exempted from control by the market (and its laws of supply and demand) and made subject to a process of political decision making? What principles have informed this decision-making process, and how can we explain the considerable variation to be found in the pension practices of contemporary capitalist democracies?

These are among the more important questions I have attempted to answer in this volume. They are, I would contend, key questions for both social gerontology and political sociology. To understand old age as it is lived today, we must transcend the ethnographic description of the many individual expressions of this experience (even those descriptions based on national surveys) and link it to the institutional structures that provide its content. The institution that now provides its economic content and material base is the welfare state.

If an understanding of the welfare state is essential for understanding old age, it is also the case that an understanding of old age is central to the enterprise of those political theorists who are engaged in explaining the welfare state. This is simply because the contemporary welfare state in the capitalist democracies is largely a *welfare state for the elderly*. In the decades following World War II, welfare-state expenditures not only grew, but grew in a particular way. The result is that expenditures on the elderly are now the largest component of the welfare-state budget. Moreover, the welfare politics of the future will increasingly be shaped by the "graying" of the state budget (Hudson, 1978) as the populations of these nations continue to age.

Chapter 1 of this volume examines the scope and the importance of today's public-pension systems for the elderly, both for the elderly themselves and for the larger public economy. It begins, however, by identifying the historical foundations of this "welfare state for the elderly" in a set of historical transformations in the development of industrial capitalism. These changes created a demand for the retirement principle and, hence, a system of retirement pensions.

Chapter 2 documents the search for a set of principles to guide the distribution of old-age pensions, principles that would enable the state to reconcile the contradictory requirements of a market economy on the one hand and a democratic polity on the other. In Chapter 3, cross-national differences in the manner in which these principles have been implemented in the capitalist democracies are examined. In Chapter 4, I draw upon main currents in contemporary political sociology in order to explain the considerable differences that exist in the quality of public pensions for the elderly in these nations. Chapter 5 concludes this analysis with an examination of the current crisis in old-age security. Here, I depart from conventional, demographic analyses of the crisis and argue that the future of old-age security will be determined by the eventual political realignments of a post-Keynesian political economy.

Throughout this book, the analyses are both historical and comparative. They are historical because the explanation of any social structure requires consideration of the process by which it was generated; they are comparative because neither generalization nor identification of that which is unique to a given system can be achieved without such comparison. I restrict my attention, however, to the advanced capitalist democracies, not only for reasons of empirical expediency (data are more readily accessible) but also for reasons of theoretical tractability. Public pensions are the output of a political process. And while other nations have developed similar public pension systems, it is clear that the political process shaping their content and form is quite different from that of the capitalist democracies. Identical outcomes do not imply a corresponding similarity in the process producing these outcomes in either the natural or the social sciences.

Clearly, however, designation of the Western industrialized nations as *capitalist democracies* is not a theoretically innocent choice of terms. By attaching analytical importance to the term *capitalism*, I set myself apart from an important theoretical perspective holding that the motor of Western history is to be found in the concept of *industrialization*. The fact that some industrialized countries also happen to be capitalist is, in this perspective, of only minor importance for understanding modern societies. Similarly, by attaching analytical importance to *democracy*, I set this analysis apart from a theoretical tradition that, at least since Lenin, has dominated Marxist analyses of the state in capitalist society. In this tradition, democratic political institutions are little more than a "political shell" (Lenin) for what in the final analysis is simply a capitalist state that operates on behalf of capital, if not at its behest. The point of view adopted here is that the social dynamic of modern Western societies is a product of what are ostensibly the two main pillars upon which these societies are built: a capitalist economy and a democratic polity. The source of dynamism and change in these societies is to be found in the fact that these two forms of social organization represent contradictory rather than complementary principles of social participation and distribution. Among the offspring of this union of opposites is the welfare state, including old-age pensions, the ambivalences of which I have attempted to capture with the expression "citizen's wage."

At the present time, public pension policy is more than an apt topic for scholarly investigation and debate; it is also a subject of heated public controversy and political confrontation. The informed citizen attempting to reach some judgment on these issues is confronted with the often arcane technical language in which the debates on this topic are conducted and the contradictory claims of the technical experts who speak it. With respect to the first difficulty, I have attempted wherever possible to translate these technical issues into what I hope is the more familiar language of contemporary political discourse. Such a strategy is not always successful, since the language of politics also has its own syntax and vocabulary. But it provides, I would contend, a more appropriate language for discussion of these issues, since ultimately the choices to be made are political in character, a fact often concealed by the technical terminology in which they are presented. With respect to the second difficulty, I can offer the reader less comfort. Occasionally, the competing claims of the experts are matters of fact which can be ajudicated by careful analysis. Ultimately, however, the current conflict over the future of old age security is a conflict between competing social forces and the visions they carry of the good society. While I have not attempted to conceal my own preferences in this regard, I cannot pretend to resolve this issue for the reader. Instead, I hope that the analyses offered here will clarify the nature of this confrontation and aid the reader in arriving at his or her own conclusions about the future of old age in the welfare state.

Chapter

1

The Aged in the
Welfare State

Among the significant political events of 1981 was the accession to power of new political regimes in two of the world's most important capitalist democracies. In the United States, the conservative administration of Ronald Reagan came to power, bent on dismantling the American welfare state; in France, the Socialist party under François Mitterrand assumed the reins of government and, with equal vigor, began to expand France's social security system. In both nations, national social policies for the elderly were the subject of immediate attention. Turning his back on his campaign promises, President Reagan announced that it would be necessary to slash Social Security in order to save it. At the same moment, the French Socialists were announcing increases in pension benefits and a reduction in the age of retirement from 65 to 60.

The alacrity with which these two administrations set out to reform their national social programs for the elderly might appear surprising, especially in view of the other major issues facing their national economies—massive inflation, high unemployment, and a general decline in economic growth. But in fact, the reform of social policy for the elderly constituted a core element of their respective strategies for resolving these economic problems. The Mitterrand legislation represented a two-pronged attack on the country's unemployment rate. Lowering the retirement age would remove a large number of older workers from the labor force, opening up their jobs for younger workers; benefit increases, it was hoped, would stimulate demand and create more jobs. Among the Reaganites, however, such strategies were perceived as the cause rather than the cure for the problems of the United States. The welfare state had become a fetter on the market, and it would have to be dismantled to get the U.S. economy rolling again. Moreover, as the neo-conservative journals and the business press had been pointing out for almost a decade, the modern welfare state was in large measure a *welfare state for the elderly*: social expenditures on the elderly had become the largest component of the welfare-state budget. Hence, to dismantle the one it would be necessary to dismantle the other. And, in view of the anticipated rise in the size of the elderly population, the reform of Social Security would have to begin immediately to avoid an even more explosive expansion of the welfare-state budget in the future.

To address this problem, the Reagan advisers advanced two types of solutions. The first was to cut benefit levels, if not for current beneficiaries, then at least for the elderly of the future. But on this issue, the administration was soon to learn another important lesson: in recent years, old age had become *old age in the welfare state*. In all capitalist democracies, public pensions along with health care, housing, and other public entitlements now provide the material base that determines the life chances and opportunities available to individuals at the end of the economic life cycle. In the United States, as elsewhere, the majority of the elderly now depend on such benefits for most of their income. The widespread reaction against benefit cuts by both young and old reflected this fact.

The second solution illustrates an equally important feature of old age in the current period. If benefits could not be cut, it was pointed out, similar objectives could be achieved by reducing the number of beneficiaries (Clark and Barker, 1981). This goal could be accomplished by raising the age of eligibility, say from 65 to 68. With a stroke of the legislative brush, the size of the "elderly" population in the United States would be reduced, bringing a corresponding reduction in old-age expenditures. Conversely, the Mitterrand legislation, by lowering the age of retirement for French workers, had the immediate effect of increasing the size of France's "elderly" population. As these events illustrate, the "elderly" in modern societies depend on the state not only for their subsistence but also for their existence; by virtue of controlling access to old-age entitlements, the state also controls access to the ranks of the elderly. The aging process and the national age structure are now matters determined by public policy.

This state of affairs represents a unique turn of events in the history of old age, the result of the unfolding of two separate but closely related processes. The first such process was the gradual adoption and spread of the retirement principle—the labor practice of superannuating elderly workers at a fixed age without regard to physical or mental capacity. Until this practice became common, "old age" in its modern sense simply did not exist. In the past, those who were chronologically old did many things—they became grandparents and widows; they became sick, disabled, and unemployed. But, except for the wealthy, they did not *retire*—that is, withdraw from economic activity in advance of physiological decline. Only in the twentieth century did such a practice become common; and only since World War II has it become virtually universal.

But for retirement to become the universal condition of the elderly required a second development: the creation of a *retirement wage*. A variety of social provisions were available to the elderly in the past, but only recently has it become the purpose of such provisions to make work unnecessary and retirement possible. And in all capitalist democracies, primary responsibility for establishing and administering the retirement wage has fallen on the state. Neither personal savings nor the emergent system of employer pensions has proven adequate to the task. Instead, national programs of age-based income entitlements were created, and the majority of the elderly now depend on these programs for their livelihood. Irrespective of national differences in political systems and prevalent ideologies regarding the role of the government, the economic well-being of the elderly in the advanced capitalist democracies is the outcome of a political process. This is the key fact that now distinguishes the economic character of old age.

The result of this double development was the creation of a new social category which, by virtue of its universality, is unique in world history—a population of elders still fit for production who do not engage in economic activity. Together the spread of the retirement principle and the growth of the welfare state have transformed the very meaning of old age in the twentieth century.

Industrial Capitalism and the Older Worker: The Origins of Retirement

In the past, the situation of those who reached an advanced old age was typically like that of the elderly in colonial America, where, in Fisher's (1978: 4) words, "Most men worked until they wore out." Retirement from economic activity in advance of physiological decline was a privilege of wealth, not the universal condition that now marks entry into the ranks of the elderly. During the formative years of industrial capitalism, a similar situation prevailed. According to Achenbaum's (1978) estimates, there was little change in the labor force participation of elderly males during America's period of rapid industrialization in the late nineteenth century. In France, the labor-force participation rate of elderly males was 73 percent at the turn of the century (Guillemard, 1980: 21) and was higher among urban workers than among rural agricultural workers (Stearns, 1976: 44). Beveridge (1930: 122–23) presents data indicating that the average age of retirement among British industrial workers actually increased between 1885 and 1910.

The reasons for this continuity with the past have to do with the forms of economic organization that characterized nineteenth-century capitalism. As Mills (1951: 5) observed, the nineteenth-century North American urban worker "was no factory employee: he was a mechanic or journeyman who looked forward to owning his own shop." This was the world of the old middle class—farmers, merchants, craftspeople—in which "four-fifths of the free people who worked owned property" (Mills, 1951: 5). For the elderly, ownership of productive property meant that retirement involved two separate processes, the first related to withdrawal from economic activity and the second to the transmission of productive resources (the family farm or business) to the younger generation (Goody, 1976: 119). The individual could control the timing and the pace of withdrawal from work and could also continue to exploit ownership rights to obtain an income even as control was being passed on to the young.

Older factory workers also enjoyed a modicum of job security during this period. The early factory did not abolish the traditional age-graded system of craft production but simply brought it inside the factory gates (Clawson, 1980). During this initial period, employers continued to rely on the knowledge and expertise of the traditional craftspeople. Accompanying this reliance was the survival of a pre-capitalist, paternalistic ethos that required employers to assume responsibility for the protection and support of their older workers (Bendix, 1956; Haber, 1978; Pentland, 1981). As a consequence, most workers continued in employment until death or disablement.

It would be a mistake to romanticize the situation of the elderly worker during this transitional period in the development of modern capitalism. While ownership of property was more widespread than today and labor practices provided some security to the aging employee, this security was limited by a low standard of living and by fluctuations in the business cycle that brought long periods of economic stagnation. Nonetheless, until the turn of the century, the problem of old age was largely defined in relation to those elderly persons who through chance and circumstance possessed neither jobs nor property (Haber, 1978). In the decades that followed, however, attention began to shift from the few elderly who were not employed to the many who were. As industrial capitalism matured, a new problem was discovered—the problem of the older worker.

In Graebner's (1980) account, it was Sir William Osler, physician-in-chief at the Johns Hopkins University Hospital, who first brought the problem of the older worker to public attention. In his valedictory address at Johns Hopkins in 1905, Osler proclaimed the uselessness of men above 40 years of age. "Take the sum of human achievement in action, in science, in art, in literature—subtract the work of the men above forty," he announced, "and while we should miss great treasures, even priceless treasures, we would practically be where we are today" (quoted in Graebner, 1980: 4). Osler stopped short of recommending retirement for all men above 40, but for those above 60 retirement was imperative if the "many evils" perpetuated by those who continue working during their seventh and eighth decades were to be avoided. For Osler, the elderly were an obstacle to achieving the potential inherent in a maturing industrial order.

Though Osler's views of the older worker initially received quite a bit of adverse comment, they quickly became accepted as established wisdom. In part, this was due to a growing recognition that soon there would be more older workers. The phenomenon of population aging had begun to appear in Sweden and France in the nineteenth century and in the twentieth century became a characteristic feature of all industrializing countries (see Table 1.1). By the 1920s, speculation about the threats to economic prosperity and political stability that would be produced by a "nation of elders" began to appear with increasing regularity in the popular and the academic press (Achenbaum, 1978: 114).

By World War II, the problem of population aging had become firmly linked to the problem of productivity. In a report prepared for the League of Nations in anticipation of postwar labor requirements, population aging was seen as a major problem for the industrial economies, where maximum productivity was thought to be reached by "men under 35" (Notestein et al., 1944: 130). In contrast, the aging of the work force was considered to be less of an obstacle in the agricultural regions of Southern and Eastern Europe, since agriculture "is an industry in which worker efficiency is retained with age" (Notestein et al., 1944: 130). In 1948, the prominent French demographer Alfred Sauvy argued that economic stagnation would follow the "demographic stagnation" of an aging society. Entrepreneurship would suffer because the energetic section of the labor force (that is, the young) would be denied access to the positions of power and influence necessary to exercise their creative faculties (Sauvy, 1948).

Theoretically, it is not especially difficult to determine why the older worker should come to be thought of as a problem in a modern capitalist economy. Ben Franklin expressed the essence of the "spirit of capitalism" in his famous aphorism, "time is money." It is instructive to consider why this is the case and how it affects the situation of the older worker. This can best be done by analyzing the

Table 1.1
Percentage of Population over 65, Selected Countries, 1850–1970

	England and Wales	France	Germany	Italy	The Netherlands	Sweden	United States	Canada
1850	4.6	6.5			4.7	4.8		
1900	4.7	8.2	4.9		6.0	8.4	4.1	5.1
1930	7.4	9.3	7.4	6.2	6.2	9.2	5.4	5.6
1950	10.8	11.8	9.7		7.7	10.3	8.1	7.8
1969–70	13.0	13.0	14.0	11.0	10.0	14.0	10.0	8.0

Source: Peter Laslett, "Societal Development and Aging," in R. Binstock and E. Shanas (eds.), *Handbook of Aging and the Social Sciences* (New York: Van Nostrand Reinhold Co., 1976), p. 103.

relations of production under merchant capitalism. The merchant capitalist of the pre-industrial period was a trader who purchased finished products and sold them in the market. It mattered little to the merchant how much time had been required to produce the goods purchased, since the price paid to the direct producer was unaffected. Whether it took an older worker ten hours to produce what a younger worker could produce in eight was of little importance. But the creation of a labor market where labor itself became the commodity to be bought and sold changed all this. The entrepreneur no longer purchased actual labor (a finished product) but rather the worker's time (potential labor). The critical problem of such a system was that of converting this potential labor into actual labor. How much each worker produced during a fixed period of time—what we now refer to as productivity—became the crucial measure of a firm's viability in a competitive marketplace. Under such circumstances, it is not difficult to appreciate the new risk faced by older and slower workers. As Rubinow observed in 1913, the dependence of the "majority of mankind . . . upon a wage contract" meant that older workers encountered total economic disability when they fell "below the minimum level of productivity set by the employer" (quoted by Lubove, 1968: 115).

If it is easy for us in retrospect to identify the economic imperatives of a system of production based on wage labor, it was apparently more difficult for the early employers of labor (Pollard, 1964; Braverman, 1974). As purchasers of labor time, they had acquired the power and the need to organize both the labor process (the way work is done) and the labor force (who works) to ensure maximum output in a minimum period of time. But both the scale and the character of managing an industrial work force raised problems that "were new to the industrial entrepreneur, who had to deal with them as they appeared for the first time in history, and who could not in this field, as in most others, base his experience to any extent on that of the merchant or the putting-out master who proceeded him" (Pollard, 1964: 4). Consequently, the organization of the early factory remained for many years like that of the traditional workshop, where craftspeople carried out their work much as they had done in the past. So long as things remained this way, the position of the older worker remained relatively secure. By the time Osler made his speech in 1905, however, a number of forces had converged to change this situation—forces that ensured a receptive audience for his message at the peaks of society, if not at the base.

The key to these changes is to be found in the long-term process of capital concentration and centralization that by the turn of the century had largely transformed the economy from one composed of many small units of production to one composed of a few large and increasingly diversified corporate enterprises. In this greatly enlarged and more diversified workplace, responsibility for management of the work force passed from the owner-entrepreneur into the hands of the "new men of power"—the emergent managerial class created to supervise and regulate the modern corporation. The authority of this new class rested not on its ownership of capital or on the risk-taking of the entrepreneurial adventurer of the nineteenth century but rather on its capacity to *manage*—that is, to systematically apply rules of rational calculation to the maximization of corporate profit (Bendix, 1956).

This systematic search for profit led first to the redesign of the labor process—the organization of work and production. Based on the principles of scientific management outlined by Frederick Taylor, the organization of work was to be restructured to minimize the total amount of labor time (especially skilled labor time) put into the manufacture of each product. By careful analysis, Taylor argued, the good manager should be able to reduce the production process to its simplest components, thereby making it possible for each task to be carried out by even the least skilled of workers. This "deskilling" of the labor process undermined the work organization of traditional craft production previously incorporated into the factory (Braverman, 1974; Clawson, 1980). As a result, the older, more skilled workers lost the privileged position they had occupied in the craft hierarchy.

The search for efficiency did not stop with the rationalization of the labor process, however. As Taylor emphasized, a reconstituted *labor process* also required a reconstituted *labor force*—one selected according to "scientific" principles rather than custom or sentiment. Through the application of sound personnel policies, only those workers most fit for each task were to be selected, and, as Graebner (1980) documents, fitness was increasingly associated with speed. In part, this was due to earlier victories by the labor movement in winning higher wages and a shortened work day. In exchange, employers demanded the *speedup* so that the same amount could be produced in less time (Graebner, 1980: 24–27). The growing adoption of machine technology also played a role. But as Graebner (1980: 19) observes:

> it was not the technology itself, but rather the speed at which it was operated, which brought grief to the older worker. Employers apparently felt that the high capital costs of new machinery could be justified only if that machinery were operated at speeds that led inevitably to the obsolescence of workers too old to maintain required levels of productivity.

As a result, the demand for retirement as a means of absolving the enterprise of the responsibility to provide work and income for the elderly worker began to grow.

Managers were also aware that if the means could be found to institutionalize retirement they could alter not only the "stock" of labor (that is, the composition of the labor force) but also its "flow." Retirement would open up promotion opportunities for younger workers, thereby enhancing morale; skilled workers could be replaced more readily by the unskilled or by those with the new skills required by changing technology; and, where wages were linked to seniority, highly paid older workers could be replaced by less expensive younger workers.[1] The benefits to be derived from a program of obligatory retirement based on chronological age were well summarized in the report submitted by Canada's first civil service commissioner, Adam Shortt, in 1922 (quoted in Bolger, 1980: 8):

> It is believed that a superannuation scheme will prove one of the best means of promoting efficiency in the service. . . . The advantages of superannuation in the public interest are apparent inasmuch as it relieves the government of the embarrassment and extravagance of retaining the services of officers who have outlived their usefulness; creates a proper flow of promotions; renders the service more mobile; deters efficient workers from leaving the public service for private employment . . . [and] in general tends to promote efficiency in every way.

The demand for universal retirement was given added urgency by the massive unemployment created by the Great Depression. Retirement would reduce the size of the labor force and open up jobs for younger workers, who were those most likely to have dependent children to support and were also those most likely to generate social unrest.

Until the 1930s, however, other considerations competed with the retirement principle and the benefits presumed to follow from it. First, managers tended to resist adoption of Taylor's new principles, correctly perceiving them as a threat to their autonomy (Bendix, 1956), and managerial resistance was reinforced by the opposition of organized labor. Second, where the theory of scientific mangement was embraced, its principles were not strictly applied and older workers were not turned out of the workplace (Graebner, 1980: 36). In a context of increasing labor militancy, older workers were considered, correctly or not, as a source of stability and conservatism. As Graebner (1980: 40) points out, employers faced a trade-off between two kinds of efficiency—productive and social:

> the choice was usually between a stable, conservative work force that blended youth with age and produced moderate short-term efficiency,

and a more mobile, potentially more radical and militant work force made up of highly productive younger workers.

Third, the necessity of dealing with the problem of older workers by means of retirement was inversely proportional to the availability of less strenuous jobs to which the elderly could be moved as their capacities declined. In the past, employers had set aside such positions for their older workers (Haber, 1978: 84), and even as the availability of these positions declined in industry, there was a compensating increase in the rapidly expanding service sector of the economy.

What role did workers (potential retirees) play during this period? Recent accounts (Graebner, 1980; Haber, 1978) emphasize the role of societal, and especially corporate, elites in spreading the retirement principle in the twentieth century. As Haber (1978: 78) writes, "this concept did not arise from the employee, at least in private industry. Instead, it was devised and endorsed by charity reformers, large industrialists, and social and economic analysts." Stearns (1976: 46–47) concludes that retirement was completely alien to British and French working-class culture and was actively resisted by the industrial proletariat. Graebner (1980) argues that it was not until the period after World War II that the retirement principle was successfully "sold" to the U.S. working class. Union leaders in both North America and Europe frequently resisted initiatives to create public pension systems, viewing such proposals as a device to co-opt workers and bind them to the state (Stearns, 1976: 47). But the historical accounts are not all consistent. Gratton (1983), for example, concludes that organized labor and the Democratic Party were at the forefront of the old-age pension movement in Massachusetts in the 1920s. And, faced with the exhaustion of the funds of their own "friendly societies," British trade unionists began to press for a system of public pensions in the early part of the century (Gilbert, 1966).

The inconsistency in the historical record is in all probability due more to an ambiguity within the working class itself than to a lack of quality or quantity of scholarship on this subject. In view of the typical working conditions and insecurities faced by all workers during this period, it would be reasonable to expect them to have embraced the retirement principle; reasonable, that is, if in exchange for a market wage they could anticipate an income sufficient to sustain them in old age. But such was not the case. Prior to World War II, public systems of old-age support were intended to supplement, not replace, the market wages of older workers and their families. To institutionalize retirement, it was first necessary to institutionalize the retirement wage.

The Welfare State and the Older Worker: The Consolidation of Retirement

From the vantage point of the nineteenth century, the contemporary welfare state, with its broad social provision for the elderly, would appear quite remarkable. The great victory of the bourgeois revolutions that gave rise to the present period was the establishment of the "nightwatchman" state, a form of government intended to minimize the role of the state in the lives of individuals and in their economic affairs in particular. For the state to assume responsibility for the economic well-being of its citizens (especially those still able to work) was the very antithesis of the emerging capitalist order. Indeed, much of the century was spent dismantling traditional welfare provisions for those who did not work and establishing new welfare systems to enforce work norms.

As both Polanyi (1944) and Bendix (1956) have noted, the general function of welfare policy in early nineteenth-century Britain and North America was to mobilize an unwilling population to enter the nascent industrial labor force. To do so required breaking down existing attitudes and work habits. As Pollard (1964: 161) writes, "men who were non-accumulative, non-acquisitive, accustomed to work for subsistence, not for the maximization of income, had to be made obedient to the cash stimulus, and obedient in such a way as to react precisely to the stimuli provided." Welfare policy reflected this imperative. The doctrine of "less eligibility," the basis of the British poor-law reforms of 1834, specified that the relief provided was to be such that the recipient's position would always be less "eligible" (desirable) than that of the poorest worker in the labor force. To ensure this, "outdoor relief" was abolished and paupers were threatened with the poorhouse, an institution that became as characteristic of the nineteenth-century landscape as the factory (Rothman, 1971). As the British poor-law commissioners made clear, such a place was to be designed less for the relief of poverty than for the deterrence of relief. Abolishing outdoor relief and restricting welfare to the poorhouse ensured that henceforth the majority of the population would be ready and willing "to offer themselves to any employer on any terms" (Piven and Cloward, 1971: 34).

Despite the declared intention to separate the deserving poor from the undeserving poor in Canada (Splane, 1965), Britain (Bendix, 1956), and the United States (Rothman, 1971), paupers of all types were crowded together under the same roof, including orphans, the aged, vagrants, and, not infrequently, the criminal and the insane. By the turn of the century, then, the chief obstacle to the spread of the retirement principle was the absence of any institutionalized system of income provision for those who would be excluded from the labor market by virtue of the principle's adoption. As a result, after a century of dismantling the poor laws and social welfare traditions of the late feudal and mercantilist periods (Rimlinger, 1971), the welfare state had to be reinvented.

The origins of the modern welfare state are usually associated with Bismarck's introduction of national pensions and other social benefits during the 1880s in Germany. Some form of national pension legislation has been in effect in Denmark since 1891, in Austria since 1906, in Britain since 1908, in France since 1910, in the Netherlands since 1913, in Italy since 1919, in Belgium since 1924, in Canada since 1927, in the United States since 1935, and in Switzerland since 1946.

The earliest of these reforms, however, were little more than revivals of precapitalist forms of social protection, a return to the practice of providing "outdoor relief" to the indigent without the loss of citizenship entitlements that previous poor laws had required. Benefits were minimal and were designed primarily to provide subsistence to widows, orphans, and the disabled (Rubinow, 1911: 377), as well as to supplement the typically declining incomes of active older workers. Commenting on Bismarck's reforms, for example, Conrad (1982: 10) observes: "The founding fathers were explicit about the economic role of the pensions: they should supplement the small wage still earned by the old worker or contribute to the family income of the disabled. Hence, the benefits of a male worker alone were not meant to allow for running an old couple's household." Evidence of this intent is to be found in the fact that the average monthly benefit of an old-age pensioner in Munich in 1905 was 13.5 marks, significantly below the prevailing welfare (or public assistance) rate of 20 marks (Conrad, 1982: 11). In 1919, a British investigatory committee concluded that even doubling the five-shilling pension would provide an income below the individual subsistence level (Heclo, 1974: 199). Prewar public pensions, then, were a form of social assistance for the indigent, not a retirement wage for a population of superannuated elders (Donahue, Orbach, and Pollack, 1960: 342).

To the extent that the U.S. Social Security Act of 1935 was intended as a piece of "retirement legislation," designed to induce older workers to leave the labor force (Graebner, 1980), the United States may in this respect be considered a "welfare leader," anticipating postwar developments elsewhere. But as Derthick (1979: 273) points out, even in 1950 more elderly persons in the United States were receiving old-age assistance benefits than were getting old-age security benefits. And, more importantly, the average old-age assistance (OAA) payment was 70 percent higher than the average primary insurance benefit. Although predicted needs of the future were embedded in the act, the actual benefits provided by it did not yet reflect the principle of *income security* that would transform old-age assistance into a retirement wage in the postwar decades.

It was only in the context of the economic boom following World War II that the welfare state emerged in a form that represented a radical break with the past (Flora and Alber, 1981; Kohl, 1981; Heclo, 1981; Perrin, 1969). Guided by the economic principles of Keynes (see Chapter 2), governments everywhere began to assume increasing responsibility for distributing the national income (see Table 1.2). And in all countries, income transfers to the elderly constituted the major component in this development. As Table 1.3 indicates, it requires little literary license to characterize today's welfare state as a welfare state for the elderly. With the exception of Canada and Ireland, in the capitalist democracies expenditures on the elderly and the infirm made up more than 50 percent of income-maintenance expenditures by the early 1970s.

The postwar break from the past is only partially captured by the rising volume of expenditures. As will be discussed in Chapter 2, the traditional concept of public provision for the elderly as *social assistance* gave way to the notion of *social security*. No longer was it sufficient to provide a safety net for those who fell out of the market; instead, the goal became that of providing a *retirement wage* sufficient to replace the market wage. Old-age benefits should do more than prevent destitution; they should also ensure a reasonable correspondence between pre- and postretirement living standards, it was concluded. The scope

Table 1.2

Total Expenditures for Income Security Programs as a Percentage of Gross National Product, Selected Countries, 1957–1977

	1957	1966	1977
Austria	13.5	18.5	22.2
Belgium	13.1	16.4	25.4
France	14.3	16.6	26.5
Germany, Federal Republic of	16.6	18.4	26.5
The Netherlands	10.4	16.9	28.4
Sweden	10.5	14.5	30.7
Switzerland	7.6	8.9	15.5
United Kingdom	10.0	12.3	17.1
United States	5.0	7.7	13.7

Source: U.S. Senate Committee on Aging, *Social Security in Europe: The Impact of an Aging Population* (Washington, D.C.: U.S. Government Printing Office, 1981), p. 6.

Table 1.3
Expenditure on Main Items of Income Maintenance in Member Countries of the Organization for Economic Cooperation and Development, 1972 (in percent of total income-maintenance expenditure)

Country	Old-age and invalidity pensions[a]	Child allowances	Sickness cash benefits	Unemployment and related benefits	Social aid	Other
Australia (1971/72)	62.9	14.8	1.9	1.8	—	18.7
Austria (1973)	79.5	11.4	3.6	1.7	—	3.8
Belgium	52.2	21.9	15.3	5.0	2.3	3.3
Canada	39.4	8.0	3.7	26.6	(19.6)	(2.7)
Denmark	64.5	15.5	10.8	5.7	2.9	0.5
Finland	70.4	7.3	11.8	3.6	2.8	4.0
France	56.2	20.0	11.4	1.5	4.4	6.5
Germany (1973)	72.4	2.7	7.8	3.3	4.0	9.9

Ireland (FY 1971)	46.8	12.9	16.8	2.9	6.6
Italy	67.1	11.2	3.1	0.7	7.1
Japan (1973)	65.4	2.5	8.7	5.8	2.2
The Netherlands (1973)	54.3	15.1	5.2	11.7	—
New Zealand (FY)	55.9	27.5	.4	5.9	—
Norway	68.0	15.6	1.9	1.7	3.2
Sweden	61.8	14.0	3.6	3.0	0.1
United Kingdom	62.9	7.1	8.9	9.2	—
United States	73.0	—	7.1	12.1	3.8
Dispersion[b]	9.8	7.0	6.4	5.0	4.6
Average[c]	62.4	12.2	6.1	5.2	4.3

[a]Old-age and invalidity pensions include survivors', widows', early retirement, and disability pensions. Sickness cash benefits include maternity allowances and industrial injury benefits.

[b]Measured by standard deviation.

[c]Arithmetic mean.

Source: Organization for Economic Cooperation and Development, *Public Expenditure on Income Maintenance Program* (Paris: OECD, 1976), p. 20.

and level of this development will be examined in more detail in subsequent chapters, but the Danish example is reasonably typical. Between 1935 and 1970 the state pension of an elderly Danish couple as a percentage of average net wages rose from 32.7 percent to 58.6 percent (Jensen, 1981: 33).

Not surprisingly, rising entitlements for the retired produced a corresponding rise in the practice of retirement. At the turn of the century, the majority of elderly males able to work continued to do so. Typical labor-force participation rates in the industrializing countries were between 60 and 70 percent. Between 1900 and 1930, as the welfare state was being rediscovered, these levels began to decline, but they were still between 50 and 60 percent at the outbreak of the Great Depression. The 1930s was a decade of pension reform in many countries; despite an increase in the demand for labor during World War II, average participation rates had fallen to approximately 40 percent by 1950 (United Nations, 1956).[2] After 1950, however, the progression of the retirement principle was exponential. Fueled by rising Social Security benefits (Clark and Spengler, 1980: 92–96), the participation rate of elderly males in the United States fell from 46 percent in 1950 to less than 20 percent by 1976. Relative to world standards, the spread of retirement in the United States has been

Table 1.4

Percentage of Aggregate Money Income Supplied by Source, Population 65 +, Britain (1976), Canada (1975), United States (1976)

	As a percentage of total income			As a percentage of total income less earnings		
	Britain	Canada	U.S.	Britain	Canada	U.S.
Earnings	23	11	23			
Government	47	56	42/48	61	63	55/62
Employee pensions	22[a]	12	13/7	29[a]	13	17/9
Asset income		21	18		24	23
Other	8	—	4[b]	10	—	6
	100	100	100	100	100	100

[a]Includes both employee pensions and asset income.

[b]Includes 2 percent of total income derived from pensions not allocated in the original source.

Sources: Britain: Family Expenditure Survey, unpublished tables, 1976. Canada: Health and Welfare Canada, Retirement Age (Ottawa: Health and Welfare Canada, 1979). U.S.: Susan Grad and Karen Foster, Income of the Population 55 and Over, 1979 (Washington, D.C.: Social Security Administration, 1979).

slow. By 1970, the percentage of older males still in the labor force had declined to 13.4 percent in Italy, 12.6 percent in Sweden, 11.6 percent in the Netherlands, 11 percent in Germany, and 6.8 percent in Belgium. As Gaullier (1982: 176) concludes, "[in] the period following World War II, *old age became retirement*."

The remote cause of this trend can be found in the sphere of production—the transformation of the labor force from self-employment status (primarily in agriculture) to wage and salary status (Pampel and Weiss, 1983). Without the creation of the labor market and the generalized commodification of labor, retirement in its current sense could not exist. But the proximate cause is to be found in the sphere of distribution; among wage and salary workers, it was the rising entitlements made available by the state that increasingly allowed them to withdraw from the labor market before they wore out (Clark and Spengler, 1980). By 1980, the institution of retirement had been consolidated and old age had become a period in the life cycle defined and sustained by the welfare state.

Income for the Elderly in the Welfare State

The dominant role of state pensions and other transfers in providing income to the elderly is illustrated in Table 1.4, which presents data on sources of money income among the elderly in Britain, Canada, and the United States for the mid-1970s. Before we discuss Table 1.4, several explanatory notes are necessary. First, the data are for the population over the age of 65, not for the retired; thus, earnings constitute a significant portion of total income. If data were available separately for the retired or if we were to exclude the population between ages 65 and 70, among whom labor-force participation is relatively high, the significance of earnings would decline dramatically. By presenting the percentage distribution of all other income by source once earnings have been removed, the second panel of columns highlights the components of income that are not derived from continued labor-force participation. A final note concerns the estimates for the United States. Two separate estimates are presented for the categories of government transfers and employee pensions. The high estimate for government transfers is arrived at by including pensions for government employees; the low estimate is arrived at by including these benefits under employee pensions. This difficulty arises from the fact that, until recently, government employees in the United States were not covered by Social Security because the occupational plan for this category of workers was intended as a substitute for it. In the other two countries, government employees are also covered by occupational plans, but these plans presume the presence of the universal state schemes. The one is not considered to be a substitute for the other. Thus, some significant portion of the pensions paid to government employees in the United States can be considered a functional equivalent of Social Security and should be included under the category of government transfers for purposes of comparison.

The conclusion to be drawn from Table 1.4 is self-evident: in all three countries, government transfers are the primary source of money income for the elderly. When earnings are excluded, government transfers represent approximately 60 percent of all income received by the elderly. In contrast, the contribution of employee pensions is less than 20 percent, and asset income (income from investments, rents, etc.) accounts for just over 20 percent. Moreover, were we able to follow a single age group from retirement through death with longitudinal data, we would find that as each cohort ages, the importance of government transfers increases: as each year passes, the number of wage-earners declines, savings are spent, and inflation erodes the real value of both savings and private pensions (Barnes and Zedlewski, 1981). Public pensions, on the other hand, not only are protected against inflation but also tend to be adjusted upward to reflect rising living standards. And, since income data typically exclude many in-kind transfers (such as food stamps), we may safely conclude that these data systematically underestimate the real significance of the welfare state in the lives of the elderly in these countries.

Is it reasonable to assume that the patterns observed here can be generalized to the other capitalist democracies? It is probable that income data for these three countries understate the significance of government transfers elsewhere. As will be seen in Chapter 3, benefit levels in Britain, Canada, and the United States tend to be modest by world standards, so that elsewhere it is likely that governments play an even larger role in determining the economic status of the elderly. These data, then, may be considered a conservative measure of the degree to which the elderly have become dependent on state provision in the capitalist democracies. Thus, regardless of national differences in political systems and prevalent ideologies regarding the role of government, the economic well-being of the elderly in the capitalist countries is the outcome of a political process. This sets the elderly apart from the majority of the population, for whom the primary source of income is the marketplace. Although public-pension entitlements are typically linked to market criteria (years of participation in the labor force, past earnings levels, etc.) by virtue of passing through the state, they can be, and generally are, modifed in accordance with distinctly nonmarket criteria. This is the key fact that now distinguishes the economic character of old age and provides the starting point for the analysis of the chapters to follow. Differences in both the level and the distribution of economic resources to the elderly populations of the capitalist democracies are the result of a political choice.

There is no historical necessity here—only historical fact. As the retirement system has evolved, primary responsibility for determining and administering the retirement wage has been removed from the marketplace and assumed by the state. In part, this may be accounted for by the character of the market itself. In the past, there has been considerable emphasis, particularly in the Anglo-American democracies (Rimlinger, 1971), on notions of self-help and self-reliance with respect to old age—that is, that individuals should be able to provide for their old age through savings from current wages. Such views are not merely a reflection of a bygone era. In 1966, the Canadian Commission on Tax Reform remarked (quoted in Brown, 1975: 116):

> It seems to be generally argued that individuals should set aside a portion of their income in the working years to ensure an adequate command over goods and services in their retirement years. Such private provisions for retirement are thought to foster self-reliance and to reduce the need for the state to provide relief.

Reliance on personal savings from market wages, however, was clearly an unrealistic strategy if the retirement principle was to be universally adopted. For the majority of workers, the bulk of income was required simply to meet the consumption needs of daily life. Only the very highest-paid workers were able to save the amounts necessary to provide for a retirement period that spanned an ever-growing portion of the life cycle. And during inflationary periods, the real value of such savings was soon eroded, leaving even the most prudent in relative penury (Kreps, 1976). Schulz (1980: 78) estimates that it would be necessary to save 20 percent of one's earnings each and every year in the labor force to achieve a target of 60–65 percent replacement of average earnings during the last five years prior to retirement. To put the principle of self-dependence into practice would mean that today, as in the past, retirement would be a prerogative of wealth.

Private pensions have proven to be no more effective than private savings in meeting the income needs of the retired. From the turn of the century on, there has been continued expansion of private occupational pension schemes, but corporate welfare systems proved too selective and too unreliable. Prior to World War II, occupational pensions were introduced primarily as a form of labor control. As Melchers (1980: 53) points out, private pensions first began to appear in those industries (such as railways) where geographical dispersal of the work force made traditional practices of labor discipline impractical. The provision of a pension at the end of the economic life cycle was intended to produce a devoted and loyal worker and to substitute for the more direct forms of control and surveillance available in the factory. Occupational pensions were also considered a useful mechanism to reduce labor turnover and to inhibit workers' actions that were inconsistent with the interests of employers, such as union organizing and strike activity (Lubove, 1968: 129*ff.*). Pension benefits were not defined as a legal entitlement but rather as a gift of the employer, given in return for years of loyal service. The potential threat of the employer's using these discretionary powers to withhold benefits was intended to induce a cooperative frame of mind in an increasingly militant and organized labor force.

Occupational schemes were given further impetus by the wage controls and labor scarcity that accompanied World War II. Employers used various fringe benefits—but especially pensions—as a way of competing for labor, which was in short supply. After World War II, privately funded pension schemes were viewed as a means of routinizing the "propensity to save." It was Charles Wilson, chairman of General Motors, who first proposed that such a scheme be established for GM workers. The accumulated funds would benefit U.S. capital as a whole by being broadly invested in U.S. industry through the stock and bond markets.

But except in those nations where private occupational plans became the object of state intervention, the corporate welfare system was unable to create a program of income allocation for the elderly of either the scope or the quality necessary for the universal practice of retirement. The major obstacle was the inability of the private sector to provide adequate coverage of the labor force. By the onset of the Great Depression, only one-eighth of all manufacturing employees in the United States were covered (Lubove, 1968: 127). Even by 1980, less than half of the labor force was covered by private occupational plans in Canada and the United States. In Europe, coverage levels of 70 percent or more have become commonplace, in part because of state intervention and state subsidies (such as in Britain) that remove the risks associated with administering a private income-maintenance system. Such schemes are basically state systems administered in the private sector. West Germany continues to function with a genuine private system that covers the majority of workers, but this system provided a trivial 6.3 percent of all pension benefits in 1976 (U.S. Department of Health and Human Services, 1980: 2).

In addition to the problem of coverage, there was the problem of reliability of corporate pension plans as a source of income security in old age for those who were covered. Workers had no assurance of actually receiving a pension. Pension rights could be lost as a result of job changes, employer discretion, or pension-fund failure (a not uncommon occurrence during the Depression years). Wars, depression, and periods of massive inflation demonstrated that the market was a place for risk-taking and not for the provision of income security. Even without the financial ruin brought on by depression and wars, the market was helpless in the face of inflationary pressures. Unlike the state, which by means of its power to tax is able to recapture the real wealth that is redistributed by inflation, the private pension market has been unable to provide an inflation-free investment vehicle to prevent significant erosion of real income over the retirement period (Pesando and Rea, 1977; Myles, 1981). As a result, while private occupational schemes remain a significant source of income for the elderly, primary responsibility for retirement wages now rests with the state.

If the market was unable to meet the needs of the elderly, what of the family? Research on family support for the elderly has generally tended to confirm Simmons's (1960: 65) conclusion that direct economic expressions of filial piety vary directly with "the amount of persuasion or coercion that may be exerted on the young and strong to serve and pay homage to the needs and interests of the old and physically feeble." Historically, the capacity of the elderly to exert control over the young has reflected prevailing patterns of economic dependency of the young upon the old. In the agrarian economies of pre-industrial Europe and North America, the entrenched property rights of the elderly and the dependence of the young on their anticipated inheritance of this property to gain their own livelihood provided, in Goody's (1976: 118) words, "both a carrot for the young and a surety for the old." Typically, the transmission of control over the family farm or business was accompanied by a legal contract obliging the heirs to provide lifelong support for their aging parents (Goody, 1976; Haber, 1978). But as Simmons (1960: 77) observes:

> whenever the existing property of a society becomes concentrated into the hands of a very small proportion of the population, and without adequate means of redistribution, its effectiveness as a means of participation for the majority of old people is greatly diminished. If concentration of property ownership is carried too far, large numbers of old people will become very dependent in an otherwise rich society.

This, of course, is precisely what characterized the transition from nineteenth-century entrepreneurial capitalism to twentieth-century corporate capitalism. As independent commodity producers (farmers, craftspeople) and small merchants were transformed into wage and salary workers, the customary bases of gerontocratic power were eroded. In contemporary societies, the majority of the young are dependent on the labor market and not on their family of origin to gain a livelihood. Family resources are transmitted primarily through differential access to education and social skills that enhance the individual's ability to compete in the labor market. Since these opportunities occur relatively early in the family life cycle, however, they do nothing to enhance the power of the elderly. We must be precise about the character of this development, though, for it is not the case that the young no longer support the elderly. What has changed is the social organization of this support: responsibility for the aged has been removed from the confines of the family, and the risks associated with support of the elderly have been collectivized in the welfare state.

Conclusion

In the language of C. Wright Mills (1959: 8), aging and old age have long since been a source of "private troubles." Faced with declining capacities and resources on the one hand and confronted with the threat of impending death on the other, men and women throughout history have been preoccupied with discovering the secret to a happy old age. But now old age has also acquired the status of a public issue, one that transcends the localized environment of self, family, kin, and community. As the examples of the Mitterand and the Reagan administrations illustrate, aging and old age have become core issues for both the economy and the polity. In turn, growing old has become an experience that is defined and sustained by the principles of labor-force management that guide the economy and by the political principles that influence the practices of the contemporary welfare state.

This simple fact poses an enormous challenge to social gerontology, because to understand the contemporary character of old age we must understand the institutions that now shape this experience and provide its material base. If in the past the social character of old age was structured at the micro level by family, kin, and community, then today it is structured at the macro level by the same institutions that set national economic objectives and defense policies and regulate foreign relations. As a result, a political sociology of aging and old age becomes a *sine qua non* for any adequate account of old age today. This requires much more than the analysis of the role of "gray lobbies" in the political process or whether political behavior is altered by aging. Until the modern welfare state created the elderly as a distinct political constituency, the elderly as elderly played only a marginal role in shaping the policies and practices that now affect their lives (Heclo, 1974; Derthick, 1979). Hence, it is necessary to go far beyond the gerontologist's usual concern with the elderly as such to examine the institutions and processes that shape the contemporary experiences of growing old.

This does not imply that a political sociology of aging must now be created *ex nihilo*. While national and comparative studies of the public policies for the aged are still few in number (Aaron, 1967; Heclo, 1974; Estes, 1979; Guillemard, 1980; Derthick, 1979), the larger body of both theoretical and empirical work that subsumes such policies is now vast indeed. For at least two decades now, the various analytical frameworks of political theory have been applied with regularity and diligence to the study of the welfare state, and, as we have seen, public expenditures on the elderly are the single largest item in the budgets of the existing welfare state. It is from within this broader tradition in political and social theory that any analysis of the politics of aging must begin. But where are we to begin?

In Chapters 3 and 4 we shall turn to the important task of identifying and explaining the considerable variation that exists in the policies and practices of the contemporary capitalist democracies with respect to the elderly and the retired. But before doing so we must establish the limits within which such variations occur. While there are important differences in the quantity and quality of social entitlements for the elderly in the advanced capitalist democracies, these are largely variations on a common theme. This commonality reflects the underlying identity of the structural limits imposed by the political and economic institutions of these countries on both policy makers and the policy-making process. If politics is the art of the possible, then it is first necessary to determine the structural boundaries that delimit the possible. And, since social policies for the elderly—whether in the field of pensions, health care, or social services—are ultimately distributional policies, it follows that we must begin by concerning ourselves with the limits that the core institutions of modern societies place on the distributional choices available to the policy makers and managers of the welfare state.

Notes

1. In some cases, a semblance of the old order was maintained by the adoption of the seniority principle. But because older workers were generally highly paid, this only stimulated the search for an alternative means for their exclusion (Haber, 1978: 85).
2. The effects of the Social Security Act of 1935 have been demonstrated by Gratton (1981). Whereas average participation rates for elderly males in U.S. cities fell at an average rate of 2 percent per decade between 1890 and 1930, during the following two decades they fell at an average rate of 7 percent per decade.

Chapter

2

Social Protection in
the Liberal Democratic State

The transformation of old age in the twentieth century was accompanied and made possible by the creation of a system of income distribution to provide for retired workers in their old age. And, as we have seen, responsibility for the development and administration of this distributional system fell for the most part upon the state. But any system of distribution requires principles to determine how much will be distributed and to whom. In the labor market, this distributional process and the structure of inequality it produces are, in theory, determined only by the market's own laws of supply and demand. The laws of the labor market, however, do not solve the problem of how income is to be distributed to non-producers—groups such as the elderly who have left the labor force. Thus, when the state assumed responsibility for the creation of an alternative distributional system, it simultaneously assumed the task of creating a set of rules to direct this activity. The amount each individual would receive after retirement was to be determined as a result of a political process in which individual entitlements would be registered a priori in a set of formal rules and regulations. Rather than being unconsciously structured by the invisible hand of the market, income inequality in old age became consciously structured by the state.

Despite the variety of principles that were adopted in various places and at various times, the characteristic form that social benefits for the elderly eventually acquired in all of the advanced capitalist countries is that of a *citizen's wage*. The citizen's wage is the hybrid offspring of the marriage of two contradictory logics of distribution and participation that became wedded in the liberal democratic state. By virtue of its liberalism, the state incorporated into its distributional system the wage-based inequalities of a capitalist economy. The income provided at the end of the economic life cycle came to be defined as a deferred wage, the value of which depended on the earned wage set by the market. But because it was subject to the control of the democratic state, the final value of this deferred wage was not limited by the market. For in their capacity as citizens, workers were able to lay claim to a share of the social product over and above any claims they may have possessed in their capacity as wage earners.

The story of the evolution of the citizen's wage is a story of convergence. From very disparate origins, the public pension policies of the advanced capitalist countries in the twentieth century converged on a set of distributional principles that are remarkably similar. This similarity is neither accidental nor merely the result of cultural diffusion; rather, it reflects the essential identity of the underlying structural bases (both economic and political) that have set limits on and guided the formation of old-age pension legislation. This convergence at the level of principle of course does not imply a corresponding convergence at the level of practice—a subject to be pursued in subsequent chapters. Although in all countries the citizen's wage bears the genetic traits of both its parents, the actual mix of these traits can and does vary considerably. But before examining the variations within a species, it is essential to identify that which is species-specific. A historical perspective is necessary to achieve this end, for it is in the evolution of a species that its basic structure is produced and given form.

The Dialectics of Distribution in the Liberal Democratic State

In a remarkable essay first presented at Cambridge in 1949, British sociologist T. H. Marshall depicted the arrival of the modern welfare state as the culmination of an evolutionary process that traced its roots to the eighteenth century. In Marshall's view, the search for social equality that produced the welfare state in the twentieth century was but "the latest phase of an evolution of citizenship which had been in progress for some 250 years" (Marshall, 1964: 78). The *social rights* of protection from economic insecurity and a modicum of economic welfare for all were now added to the *civil rights*, including freedom of speech and equality before the courts (which were fought for and won in the eighteenth century), and to the *political rights* of voting and participation in the exercise of power (achieved during the struggles of the nineteenth century). But for Marshall, the emergence of citizenship as a basis of social organization during this particular historical period was a curious paradox because it coincided exactly with the rise of capitalism—"a system, not of equality, but of inequality" (1964: 92). This marriage between a protective state and a capitalist economy was a union of opposites, for it required an accommodation between two opposing logics of distribution—one that attached rights to the possession of *property* and another that attached rights to *persons* in their capacity as citizens. Moreover, it was a union fraught with conflict and struggle. As Marshall (1964: 93) observed, throughout the twentieth century, citizenship and the capitalist class system had been at war. And, as Alan Wolfe (1977) has argued, the structural basis for this war lay inside the liberal democratic state itself.

The liberal state, born of the bourgeois revolutions, was a state in which political participation and individual rights were based on economic capacity and the ownership of property. In contrast, the democratic state was the product of a century of struggles by workers for political representation on the basis of citizenship—that is, on the basis of membership in a social community (Therborn, 1977). The result of these conflicts was that the "classical liberal state, which vested rights of political participation in owners of *property*, gave way to the liberal democratic state, which vests those rights in *persons* by virtue of citizenship" (Bowles and Gintis, 1980: 11). In adopting democratic principles of participation and distribution, however, the state did not abandon its liberalism. Rather, these two opposing doctrines were subsumed within a single structure, thereby producing the internal tension which provided the source of its own evolution and transformation.

For the liberal state, the key tenet to be observed in the development of social policy was that such policies be market-conforming. In particular, these policies should do nothing to undermine the foundation of capitalist social relations—namely, the commodity character of labor. Social benefits could be provided outside of the market, but they always had to be a mirror image of the relative prices (wages) assigned by the market to each individual's labor power. Any policy that undermined the "natural" process of wage determination in the market was unacceptable. But the distributional logic of the democratic state was quite the opposite. In the democratic state, rather than representing commodities of unequal value, individuals met as equal citizens, as members of a community in which the criterion of need as well as of equity could and should be recognized. As such, the democratic state constantly threatened to decommodify labor, to provide individuals and families with the means to maintain a normal standard of living independently of their position in the labor market (Esping-Andersen, 1981: 11).

Since the structural and ideological conditions necessary for the creation of the market economy and the liberal state were established with great difficulty, it is not surprising that subsequent efforts to create social institutions that undermined or even appeared to undermine these conditions encountered considerable opposition. From the point of view of the ascendent bourgeoisie, state provision for the elderly and the disabled that could not be justified according to the criteria of the market looked remarkably like a return to the feudal and mercantilist practices they had fought so hard to overthrow or like the first step toward socialism. The whip hand of the market would be softened as individuals came to recognize that there would be other sources of income when they were unable to provide for themselves. As an anonymous "Yorkshire liberal" observed in 1908: "Once a wage is conceded beyond the economic value of the labor as a moral right . . . you cannot stop at any particular figure but give away the whole case against socialism" (quoted in Wolfe, 1977: 78).

State pensions for the elderly were often opposed with equal vigor by organized labor and by the left. For those Marxists who viewed the liberal state as little more than the executive committee of the ruling class, any increment in state power meant an increase in the power of capital over labor. In addition, early state initiatives were frequently in direct competition with labor-organized insurance schemes. Such schemes had the dual advantage of being under the direct control of workers and of attracting workers to the labor movement.

Thus, for both classical liberalism and classical Marxism, expansion of state control in any sphere of life was a development to be opposed. For nineteenth-century liberals, state control meant undermining the market; for socialists, it meant enhancing the power of the bourgeois state and capitalist social relations in general. As we shall see shortly, both sets of fears proved to be only partially substantiated, reflecting the contradictory forces guiding the policy-making process inside the liberal democratic state. As subsequent years have demonstrated, it is not state control as such that matters, but how that control is exercised. The fact that the wages of the elderly were removed from the market and administered by the state did not mean that the state could not use this power to produce a system of income distribution that would reflect and even reinforce the market. Indeed, it was quite possible for the state to behave as though it were a capitalist firm, and national social security systems could be run as if they were simply large, monopolistic insurance companies.

But despite the liberal state's capacity to recognize and adopt the criteria of the market, once it also became a democratic state it became subject to a competing logic of distribution. Whereas the inherent justice of the benefits provided by a life annuity purchased in the marketplace could never be questioned on the grounds that those benefits did not satisfy the economic needs of the beneficiary, "meeting unmet needs" frequently became a perfectly acceptable criterion of decision making inside the democratic state. An annuity purchased in the market is a commodity like any other, with its price and value determined by strict market practices. When that same annuity is produced within the political sphere, it is possible—but by no means necessary—that such be the case. And, indeed, modifications of market entitlements on the basis of need have become the norm, not the exception. Allowances for dependents, widows' benefits, and ad hoc adjustments to deal with unexpected economic and political catastrophe have all become commonplace within developed state pension systems.

The result of this compromise between the demands of liberalism and those of democracy produced a hybrid system of public pensions that appears to many to lack any internal consistency or logic whatsoever. From the right, the system continues to be attacked for departing from strict principles of equity (to each according to his or her contributions), and the system is criticized from the left for being regressive and for failing to contribute to greater equality (to each according to his or her needs). But as Marshall observed (1964: 133), this apparent lack of consistency is a source of befuddlement only to those who think that social behavior is governed by logic. The conflict of principles that became embodied in the modern welfare state reflects not "the muddled thinking of our rulers," he wrote, "but, rather, springs from the very roots of our social order in the present phase of the development of democratic citizenship."

Hence, just as the demand for the retirement principle was an essential byproduct of the evolution of the labor practices of the capitalist firm, so too was the citizen's wage a systemic effect of the rise of the liberal democratic state which accompanied this evolution. But the citizen's wage was the end product of this process. We must now step back in time and examine its origins.

The Commodification of State Pensions: Germany and the United States

In the timing and the circumstances of their formation, the public pension systems of Germany and the United States represent contrasting poles in the evolution of the modern welfare state. Germany was the first country to introduce national compulsory old-age insurance in 1889. The United States was among the last of the industrialized nations to do so. Bismarck's reforms were adopted as a tool to assist in the industrialization process; Roosevelt's Social Security Act of 1935 came after the industrialization of the U.S. economy was virtually complete. Bismarck's intent was to preserve the patriarchal tradition of the old order within an industrialized economy; Roosevelt intended to save a modern capitalist social order from destruction. As Alan Wolfe (1977: 50) remarks, "Bismarck's 'welfare' state was a glance not to the future but to the past; it is closer in conception to Speenhamland than to the New Deal." Unlike the Social Security Act of 1935, which was intended to induce older workers out of the labor force and into retirement, the German legislation was primarily a reflection of the tradition of the poor laws, providing a subsistence income when the worker became disabled and giving support to the family when the worker died. Bismarck sought to provide a political solution to a political problem, to provide social protection in exchange for social harmony and the maintenance of the old order. Roosevelt also sought to restore social peace in the face of the mass turmoil produced by the Great Depression. But the Social Security Act was not simply an exercise in political engineering; it involved economic engineering as well (Graebner, 1980). The income-maintenance system for the elderly was designed to remove older workers from the labor force, thus freeing jobs for younger workers and reducing the unemployment that was the source of the turmoil.

In other respects, however, these first efforts at implementing social legislation for the elderly in Germany and the United States were remarkably similar. In both cases, the national bourgeoisie found itself in a weak position inside the state. In Germany, which had never experienced a bourgeois revolution, the state was dominated by a traditional "dynastic elite" (Kerr et al., 1964: 37) that was assisted by a strong, disciplined bureaucracy. In the United States of the Great Depression, the capitalist order was under attack, capitalists were on the defensive, and a strong centralized state bureaucracy was in the process of being formed to deal with the crisis produced by the failure of the economy. But despite this temporary lack of esteem and formal control of the state apparatus, it was the liberal ethos of the national bourgeoisie that left the most lasting imprint on both nations' legislation for the elderly. State provision for the elderly was to become an adjunct of the market, reflecting its rules of distribution, rather than an alternative to it.

The German reforms of 1889 (by which compulsory old-age insurance and insurance for invalids were introduced for the working class) were both a response to the forces of democratization and an attempt to suppress them.[1] In an effort to contain the new industrial order within the traditional structure of political privilege, Bismarck sought to diffuse the demands for *political* rights coming from a radical and increasingly well-organized working class. He would achieve this by providing *social* rights that would tie the worker to the state rather than to the worker's class. During this period, the electoral strength and the political influence of the socialists were on the rise. Between the first elections to the Diet of the new German empire in 1871 and the elections of 1877, they increased their share of the vote from 3 to 9 percent and increased their elected members from two to twelve. In order to check this development, Bismarck responded with a dual strategy of repression and bribery. Repression came in the form of a bill banning the Social Democrats from electoral participation. But at the opening of the Reichstag in February of 1879, the Emperor announced that more would be needed. He sought the cooperation of the legislature in adopting a program of social reform because, as he observed, "a remedy cannot be sought merely in the repression of Socialistic excesses—there must be simultaneously a positive advancement of the working classes" (quoted in Dawson, 1912: 12). State-provided social protection for the worker was intended to increase the workers' stake in the existing order and hence their loyalty to an autocratic but paternalistic state. As Bismarck remarked to the Reichstag on the eve of the pension reforms of 1889 (quoted in Rimlinger, 1971: 121):

> I will consider it a great advantage when we have 700,000 small pensioners drawing their annuities from the state, especially if they belong to those classes who otherwise do not have much to lose by an upheaval and erroneously believe they can actually gain much by it.

In introducing such reforms, Bismarck sought not only to check the threat of the working class but also to contain the power of the still weak but emergent bourgeoisie, whose liberal conception of the minimal state posed an equal danger to the old order. Collaboration between crown and proletariat against the liberal bourgeoisie was a notion in German political thought dating from the 1840s (Rimlinger, 1971: 100). But as Rimlinger has shown, the patriarchal tradition represented by Bismarck was successful only in affecting the introduction of a system of state pensions for the elderly; it was much less successful in shaping its content.

Bismarck was strongly opposed to the introduction of any form of insurance concept into the state schemes—that is, any mechanism that would suggest that the workers had in any way *earned* the benefits they received. As he observed, if a worker pays for his own benefits, "the effect on him will be lost" (quoted in Rimlinger, 1971: 118). A contributory scheme would negate the intent of the reforms—

namely, to create the appearance of a benevolent state that cared for its (obedient) children in times of need. But Bismarck was forced to compromise on this issue. He faced stiff opposition from those demanding that old-age insurance not undermine the liberal principles of individual responsibility and self-help. As a result, the system that became law in 1889 was funded primarily by contributions from employers and employees, and benefits were to be established in relation to the level of contributions paid into the fund. Bismarck succeeded only in incorporating a fifty-mark flat subsidy to be paid to all beneficiaries by the Imperial Treasury. Thus, despite its origins in the traditional order, the German pension legislation clearly reflected the priorities of the emergent market ethos. The state program was set up in commodity form—a service was purchased for a price reflecting the value received. By linking contributions and benefits, the state reproduced the income structure created by the market. Although provided outside of the market, state pensions for the elderly did not violate the rules of the market.

Perhaps the clearest expression of the liberal ethos in the area of pension reform is to be found in the theory of the Social Market Economy that served as the basis of German reconstruction after World War II. Immediately after the war, efforts were made to ease the plight of the aged by financing benefit increases out of general revenue, thus blurring the insurance aspect of the system. However, the major reforms of 1957 restored and reinforced the market principle by clearly separating contributory *pension insurance* from noncontributory *assistance* schemes. These reforms reflected a clearly articulated neoliberal philosophy of the role of the state in a capitalist economy. The basic concept of the Social Market Economy formulated by Alfred Muller-Armack was that state intervention would be acceptable to the extent that it was "market-conforming." In his words, "the guiding principle of social intervention in the market economy is compatibility with the functioning of market-directed production and its *corresponding income formation*" (quoted by Rimlinger, 1971: 142, emphasis added). Thus, the distributional practices of the state were to mirror those of the market. This meant that the guiding principle for passing out pension benefits was that of status preservation. State schemes would ensure that the relative economic status achieved by an individual during the work life would be preserved in old age and that the structure of income inequality created in and by the market would be reproduced as exactly as possible. There was to be no allocation on the basis of need; hence, there was to be no minimum guaranteed benefit and no provision made for dependent spouses. If the state were to intervene, it would do so following the rules of the market and would not pursue policies that might undermine or even ignore its practices.

In many respects, the national pension system for the aged introduced by Roosevelt in 1935 resembled the German legislation. Until the depression, compulsory state pensions were construed by many as something foreign and un-American, a violation of individual freedom. Bismarckian paternalism was precisely what many U.S. citizens saw lurking behind proposals for such schemes.[2] But when old-age insurance was introduced, it was not the non-contributory, flat-benefit schemes (already in existence in many European countries) that were emulated (Derthick, 1979: 218). Rather, the plan followed the German contributory and earnings-related benefit model. Apart from its obligatory nature, the old-age insurance system introduced under Title II of the Social Security Act of 1935 was constructed so as to appear to be little more than a government-administered annuity program that would run along pension principles already prevalent in U.S. industry.[3] The criterion of equity was to be strictly adhered to, with each individual receiving benefits in direct proportion to what he or she had contributed. There was no provision for dependent spouses, and widows were to be given only a lump sum that reflected the value of the beneficiary's contributions remaining at time of death. Strict market principles were to be maintained and the commodity character of the insurance contract made apparent. As in Germany, the individual was to confront the state as a consumer who had purchased a commodity, not as a citizen claiming rights as a member of the collectivity. Despite subsequent revisions that considerably weakened the equity principle and increasingly provided income on the basis of need (such as allowances for dependent spouses), great effort was put into maintaining the illusion that the state was simply acting as a large insurance company. In the words of Robert Ball (1978: 4), Commissioner of Social Security until 1973, Social Security "is a form of group insurance operated by government." To the public, at least, the program continued to be sold as a program of self-help based on individual savings. Any departure from a benefit structure based on past earnings and contributions was construed as being politically—if not morally—unacceptable (Ball, 1978: 8).

Thus, the fears of the right that any state intervention into the income allocation process would eventually lead to the destruction of the market were clearly unwarranted. In both Germany and the United States, the means by which retirement income was provided reproduced and reinforced market-based social relations in at least two ways. First, by creating a link between contributions and benefits, the state fostered the illusion that the relationship between the state and the beneficiary was simply that of a seller of a commodity and a purchaser. Second, market incentives during the work life were not reduced, since income in old age reflected past success in the market.

But just as the worst fears of the conservatives were not realized, neither were those of the left, who opposed the expansion of state power on the grounds that it represented an expansion of capitalist domination. If the market was not destroyed, it was certainly weakened, and, once brought within the state sector, the income-allocation process become subject to forces and theories quite distinct from those of the market. The reality of Social Security in the United States is such that officials have always had to devote great effort to maintaining the illusion that benefits are closely linked to contributions. Even before the initial legislation of 1935 became effective, amendments were adopted based on principles of need rather than on contributions. In 1939, an amendment was introduced to provide a supplementary benefit equal to half of the basic benefit for the support of a dependent spouse or child. If the principal beneficiary died, additional benefits were authorized for a surviving spouse and children. And in the decades that followed, increases in benefit levels were granted independently of past contribution levels. In the language of the policy makers, there was a constant trade-off between "adequacy" and "equity" (Derthick, 1979: 213). Subsequent legislation indexing benefits on the basis of price increases, in order to preserve their real value, further undermined market forces. The most important of these reforms were passed during the Nixon Administration in 1972. Likewise in Germany, the adoption of wage-based indexing meant that the retired worker was provided a share of the new wealth produced by economic growth, independent of past contributions. German legislation further compensated for the fact that certain forms of labor were undervalued in the market by establishing a minimum level for assessing benefits (Wilson, 1974: 93).

Thus, despite the time, effort, and ingenuity that went into fostering the illusion of the commodity character of public "insurance" for the elderly, it became just that—an illusion. As Derthick (1979: 224) observes of the U.S. situation: "As the link between tax payments and benefits grew more and more tenuous, the program became less and less like insurance, and the less like insurance it became, the more its executive leaders insisted that was what it was." To disarm the opponents of reform, it was important to maintain the fiction and conceal the process of decommodification taking place.

Since the state was not subject to the discipline of the market, state pensions for the elderly could potentially be organized along guidelines other than those derived from the market. The state, however, was and is, subject to the discipline of the political process.

Hence market criteria were frequently abandoned as politics required. What politics required in a formally democratic polity was that from time to time the claims of citizenship and the principle of need be acknowledged.

In Search of the Citizen's Wage

During the formative years of old-age pensions in Germany and the United States, organized labor and the left in both nations were demanding a form of social provision very different from the one that was eventually adopted. Financing, it was argued, should come from employers and from taxes on the wealthy rather than from the inadequate wages of workers. Equality and not equity should be the guiding tenet of state programs. Benefits should not reflect contributions (the equity principle of the market) but needs (the equality principle of democracy). Hence, the demand was for a similar flat benefit to be provided to all, with adjustments made to reflect the situation of households (for example, the number of dependents). Virtually identical demands were made by the Social Democrats in Germany at the end of the nineteenth century (Rimlinger, 1971: 127) and by U.S. labor (the Congress of Industrial Organizations, or CIO) in the United States in the 1930s. In 1939, the CIO called for a national program that would pay $60 per month to everyone over the age of 60 and would be financed out of taxes on income and wealth (Derthick, 1979: 113). The guiding principle was that social provision should reflect the equality of citizenship that exists among individuals in the political sphere in a democratic society, not the inequalities produced by the market. Democracy was being called upon to assert itself in the form of a citizen's entitlement to an equal share of the society's wealth.

In fact, many of the industrializing capitalist countries established similar schemes in their initial efforts to deal with the problem of old-age insecurity. Flat-benefit programs were established in Denmark in 1892, in New Zealand in 1898, in Britain in 1908, and in Canada in 1927. Initially, these were means-tested programs which provided the same minimum benefit to all citizens whose incomes fell below a stipulated level. The programs were financed from general tax revenues or earmarked flat contributions. Organized labor and left political parties were often deeply involved in the development and design of such legislation, and, in view of the stiff opposition encountered from conservative business interests and political parties, this legislation in many instances represented no small victory for the working class in these countries. The threat of impoverishment in old age was mitigated and the right to support from the community restored without the corresponding loss of the rights and privileges of citizenship that had been required under the traditional poor laws. The provision of relief was assured, and citizenship rights were not forgone as a result of such relief.

It soon became apparent, however, that these victories were only partial ones. History could not be removed with the stroke of a pen, and such provisions actually had much in common with the old poor laws. First, the stigma of the means test remained, inhibiting many from taking benefits. In practice, benefit policies could be manipulated by local authorities to serve both economic and political purposes. Thus, the elimination of the means test and the establishment of a universal program in the modern sense of the term (that is, a program that is provided to all of the elderly irrespective of other income or assets) became the major goals of subsequent reform movements. Second, as discussed in Chapter 1, benefit levels tended to fall below basic subsistence levels and in no way constituted a disincentive from continuing to work if work was available. As Heclo (1974: 195) notes with respect to the British case: "Although marking a significant break with the poor law, the 1908 act was also, as young Beveridge observed at the time, a survival of Whig orthodoxy, a special government beneficence to the needy."

Despite these shortcomings, equal benefits for all continued to be the goal of the representatives of labor and the left for a considerable period of time, and was finally given up only with great reluctance. In the long run, it became apparent that equality and capitalism were not reconcilable. Equality for the elderly too often proved to be poverty for the elderly. As a result, labor everywhere gradually began to temper its demands for strict adherence to the principles of citizenship and acknowledge the necessity of recognizing market-generated inequalities in programs of state provision for old age. The principles of citizenship would not be abandoned, but the benefits provided would be in the form of a citizen's *wage*. As an aid in understanding this evolution, it is instructive to consider several of the major postwar attempts to construct a modern welfare state on the citizenship principle. The case of Britain, where this effort was accompanied by an explicit egalitarian ideology based on the concept of citizenship, is of particular interest.

With the victory of the British Labour Party in 1945 and with the passage of such major pieces of legislation as the Family Allowances Act (1945), the National Health Act (1946), the National Insurance Act (1946), and the National Assistance Act (1948), it appeared that a new era in the history of Western capitalism had emerged. Among the English-speaking countries, the term "welfare state" was used for the first time in Britain in 1941 by William Temple, Archbishop of York

(Schottland, 1967: 16). Especially in the Anglo-Saxon world, the welfare state appeared as a distinctively radical British invention. As we shall see shortly, the actual provisions of this new legislation in the area of pension policy were not nearly so radical or so new as has frequently been assumed. What was new, however, was the understanding of state and society upon which the legislation was based. This view was articulated in the Beveridge report, a comprehensive statement on social security prepared under the supervision of Lord Beveridge and published in 1942. It was given a more refined intellectual foundation in Marshall's address in 1949 and was made acceptable to the political representatives of both capital and labor by the new economic theories of Lord Keynes.

Prepared during wartime, when the costs and risks of war were being borne by rich and poor alike, the Beveridge report became an important symbol of unification, promising a new era of collective self-help and social responsibility. It proposed a national minimum benefit to guarantee freedom from want as a right of all citizens. As Rimlinger points out (1971: 152), the provision of benefits was no longer to be a matter of providing help for the "poor" or even for the "worker"; nor was it to be predicated on either individualistic principles of self-help or paternalistic principles of dependence and protection. Rather, social protection was to be a right of citizenship in a democratic society. The state, acting on behalf of all its citizens, would provide a safety net below which no member of the community would be allowed to fall. As a result of Marshall's influential intervention, the adoption of such principles came to be seen as the natural outcome of Britain's evolution toward the full realization of citizenship.

An additional component of postwar thought that provided the framework for a new era of state intervention in the process of income allocation came from the new economic theories of Lord Keynes. What Keynes provided was theoretical justification not simply for state intervention in a capitalist economy but, more importantly, for state intervention *to redistribute income* in a capitalist economy. The problems of capitalism and capital accumulation, manifested in the business cycle, were to be resolved by stimulating consumer demand during periods of decline. This could be achieved by policies to maintain full employment (and hence to maintain wage levels) and to put money into the hands of those most likely to spend it—parents with children, the aged, etc. Provisions for the needy suddenly became *necessary* for capitalism, not a threat to its survival. As Bryden (1974: 109) observes:

> At the intellectual and policy-making level, the Keynesian revolution in economics promised the means whereby popular aspirations for a better

world could be realized. The economist's image of the economic world was basically altered. . . . Governments were now seen to have a major potential and responsibility for promoting economic growth and full employment and for providing wide-ranging social security.

With almost Hegelian elegance, the dialectic of individualism and collectivism, of capitalism and democracy had resolved itself in a new synthesis called the welfare state.

The egalitarian ethos implicit in the notion of citizenship called for a social security system in which all were treated alike. In practice, this meant that the benefits were to be the same for all, regardless of previous earnings. Similarly, the program was to be financed by equal contributions from everyone. To introduce an element of redistribution, part of the funding would come from general revenues raised from a progressive income tax. Recognizing and reproducing market inequalities was not to be the task of the state. Contributions were to be retained not for incentive purposes but rather to ensure the citizen's sense of collective participation and responsibility (Rimlinger, 1971: 151). The basic flat-benefit formula proposed by Beveridge guided postwar reforms in many countries, including Sweden (1946), Holland (1947), and Canada (1951).

But in view of the revolutionary imagery associated with it, what was most remarkable about postwar pension reform in Britain was its decidedly unrevolutionary character when put into effect. As Heclo (1974: 143) observes: "Despite all the attendant fanfare, hopes and expectations, the changes proposed by the Beveridge Report were largely ones of operational structure and not policy content." Rather than revolutionizing the system, Beveridge's safety-net approach to the welfare state did little more than formalize and systematize the practices of the prewar period. Flat-benefit, means-tested pensions had been in effect since 1908. The Widows, Orphans, and Old Age Contributory Pension Act of 1925 had introduced a flat-contribution, flat-benefit scheme that eliminated the means test, and by the end of the 1930s, approximately four-fifths of the population over 70 was receiving benefits of 50 pence per week (Kaim-Caudle, 1973: 167). Nor does the objective of increasing benefits to "subsistence" level appear to have been achieved (Heclo, 1974: 256). When the new legislation came into effect in 1948, the benefit level was only 19 percent of the average industrial wage (Heclo, 1974: 258). Rather than providing a radical departure from the market-conforming benefit structures of Germany and the United States, Beveridge simply advanced a strategy whereby the same goal could be achieved by different means. Benefits would be equal, but they would also be low; thus, they would not compete with the market as a source of income or undermine incentives to work.

It is clear that Beveridge had no intention of transforming old-age assistance into a retirement wage. In discussing the problem of old age and employment in 1945, he alluded to statistics demonstrating that the elderly were now more able than ever to support themselves by their own labor. He concluded that the "general improvement of health, which is lengthening the average total life of men, must also be helping to some extent to maintain till later their working capacity" (Beveridge, 1945: 69). But the retirement statistics to which he alluded to support this view were for the period from 1885 to 1910.

Beveridge's liberal bias was clearly expressed in the third of the three principles he prescribed as the basis for social provision: "The State in organizing security should not stifle incentive, opportunity, responsibility; in establishing a national minimum, it should leave room and encouragement for voluntary action by each individual to provide more than that minimum for himself and his family" (Beveridge, 1942: 6–7). As Marshall was subsequently to note, such provisions were a form of class abatement, not an attack on the class system. "It raised the floor level in the basement of the social edifice, and perhaps made it more hygienic than it was before. But it remained a basement and the upper stories remained unaffected" (Marshall, 1964: 95). Thus, in the postwar years old ideas paraded as reform, and the Beveridge principles served as the foundation of initial postwar pension legislation in countries as diverse as Sweden (1946) and Canada (1951).

In Canada, the major achievement of the 1951 reforms was to universalize the program that had been in effect since 1927. The means test was removed for those over the age of 70, and provisions were made to gradually lower the age for eligibility from 70 to 65. But the benefit level of $40 per month (or 17 percent of the average wage) was retained. A comparison of the plans in effect at the time in Canada and the United States shows why Canadians may have felt they were considerably better off with their flat-benefit program than with the earnings-related plan of the United States. The Canadian scheme was clearly more comprehensive in its coverage of the elderly population (a considerable number of elderly in the United States were still excluded from Social Security); and, while the maximum benefit under the U.S. system was higher than that available to Canadians, the minimum was considerably lower. Overall average benefit levels in Canada were higher than in the United States.[4] Moreover, under the Canadian system, eligibility was based only on age and citizenship. This meant that the benefit received by the dependent spouse of a retired worker was equal in value to that of the retired worker.

It was not long, however, before organized labor and the left were calling for abandonment of egalitarianism by demanding the addition of an earnings-related second tier in virtually all countries where flat-benefit systems were in effect. Just as attempts to reproduce a market-related benefit structure in the United States and Germany had been less than fully successful, so too did the pursuit of an egalitarian benefit structure, which recognized only the equality of citizenship and the principle of need, fall on hard times.

Equal but Poor

Among the major factors that led to the abandonment of the flat-benefit system was a gradual recognition that the citizen's benefit had, after all, been something of a myth. The view of equality advanced by Beveridge proved to be a double-edged sword. Under the flat-benefit structure, retired workers were equal, but they were equally poor in an otherwise wealthy society. The citizen's benefit was intended to put a floor under the market, not to replace it. The flat-benefit rates introduced in the British National Insurance Act in 1946 were below the subsistence level and remained there. That is, the rates were below the public assistance levels that could be claimed on the basis of a means test (Kaim-Caudle, 1973: 38). And workers were reluctant to leave the labor market at age 65 or 70 if it meant a substantial drop from the living standards they had achieved during their working years. The workers were usually among the first to recognize the contradiction inherent in the notion of "socialism for the elderly." Accordingly, demands for a government-sponsored pension program based on earnings were made by the Swedish Labor Organization (LO) as early as 1944, by the Canadian Congress of Labor (CCL) in 1953, and by the British Trade Union Congress (TUC) in 1957. What workers were seeking was income replacement and income security in old age, along the lines envisioned in the systems of Germany and the United States.

A second shortcoming of the flat-benefit method in a world of unequal wages was noted by Richard Titmuss and his colleagues (Heclo, 1974: 261). Rather than promoting equality, flat benefits tended over the long run to promote inequality. The reasons for this were very simple. Those workers for whom the flat benefit represented a substantial drop in living standards did not stand by waiting for the government to rectify the problem. Instead, the better organized and more powerful sectors of labor were actively pursuing private occupational schemes as part of their wage contracts. And this was precisely what had been intended. As Beveridge made clear in 1958: "State pensions should be at a basic level above which private insurance operated. . . . The individual should share some responsibility for himself and not be spoon-fed by the State" (quoted by

Heclo, 1974: 272). Support for the flat-benefit principle had been based on more than egalitarianism. It had been assumed that once the lowest-income earners had been assured of an income floor, others would make provision for their old age through pensions created in the marketplace, an assumption that won the flat-benefit method the avid support of the life insurance and trust companies (Murphy, 1982). Not only was this second tier of occupational pensions an intentional consequence of the flat-benefit policy; it also was typically subsidized by the state through fiscal policies that made contributions to such plans tax deductible. The end result, as Titmuss argued, was that the flat-benefit method created two nations of the aged—those receiving flat benefits and those receiving flat benefits plus tax-subsidized occupational pensions.

The flat-benefit principle also created impediments to the development and improvement of benefit levels in at least two other ways. First, as Titmuss pointed out, the flat-rate system effectively put a brake on the development of adequate pensions for those who needed them most, since a redistributive system of pension financing was politically unacceptable unless it was at least partially concealed within a graduated benefit structure linked to contributions. This was an outcome that apparently had been anticipated by U.S. Social Security executives (Derthick, 1979: 223). Second, what the left-wing supporters of flat benefits had failed to anticipate was the potential divisiveness of a flat-benefit system within the working class. In a world of unequal wages, equal benefits ensured that only the lowest paid and weakest sectors of the working class would have an undivided interest in the development and enhancement of the public pension system. The better paid and better organized directed their energies to enhancing the coverage and quality of private occupational pensions negotiated in wage contracts. In effect, flat benefits undercut the commitment of those sectors of labor most likely to have the political and economic clout to significantly affect the development of public pensions. As a result, the social and political divisions between the aristocrats and the underprivileged of the working class were reinforced, producing two nations among the non-elderly as well as the elderly (Furniss and Tilton, 1977: 111). As Andrew Martin (1975: 29) points out, the result of the flat-benefit method is that "public welfare institutions become less and less a system on which most members of society depend," with the consequence that "the public sector welfare state is eroded along with its universality." Things might have been different if flat benefits had not been equated with low benefits. But serious consideration was never given to a flat-benefit scheme that would set benefit levels at or near the average wage, thereby giving the majority of workers a significant stake in the system.

As the realization of the mythical character of the citizen's benefit grew and as some of its negative consequences became better understood, there was a convergence in virtually all of the advanced capitalist countries on the principles that should guide the distribution of income to the aged. The notion that an old-age benefit system should simply create a safety net to prevent absolute destitution was gradually displaced by the notion that it should provide the elderly with a reasonable standard of living. This meant that benefits should provide more than the income necessary for mere subsistence and should reflect the fact that well-being in old age requires some measure of continuity with the life-style and standard of living achieved during the working years. Accordingly, attention turned away from simply getting the elderly above the poverty line or off public assistance and increasingly focused on the problems of income replacement and income security (Perrin, 1969: 278). The latter involved consideration of two separate but interrelated aspects of pensions: (1) the level of income replacement provided at retirement (the ratio of post-retirement income assured by the pension system to pre-retirement income earned in the market), and (2) the extent to which the pension system preserved the real value of the pension over the remainder of the life cycle (the problem of indexing). Both concerns were essentially a matter of status preservation in old age. There was considerable discussion of appropriate income-replacement ratios for workers with different income levels and of what constituted an acceptable mechanism for "dynamizing" (indexing) pensions to keep up with changes in the cost of living and/or changes in the real standard of living in the society as a whole (see, for example, the comparative studies conducted by Schulz et al., 1974, and Wilson, 1974). Ironically, however, it was the inability of the market to produce a pension vehicle that could reproduce market-generated income inequalities that led the state to abandon the flat-benefit system and assume responsibility for providing the income-replacing second tier (see Chapter 1).

Perhaps the most farsighted group with respect to the inability of the private insurance market to deal with the problem of income replacement in retirement was the Swedish labor movement. As noted earlier, the Swedish LO had called for a government-sponsored earnings-related program as early as 1944. Swedish labor recognized that reliance on employers' plans would result in a failure to provide coverage for those most in need of such insurance (Heclo, 1974: 233). By the early fifties, it was also apparent that only the state could adequately deal with the problem of inflation and that reliance on the private sector could seriously divide the working class and endanger social solidarity (Heclo, 1974: 236). In 1959, under a Social Democratic administration, Sweden added an earnings-related superannuation program to the existing flat-benefit scheme.

In Canada, similar considerations of inadequate coverage and the problems arising from vesting, portability, and indexing resulted in early support for a government-administered second tier from the Canadian Congress of Labour (1953) and Canada's social democratic party, the CCF (1957). The legislation that introduced the second tier in Canada, the Canada Pension Plan (CPP) was passed under a Liberal administration in 1965. In Britain, the Conservative Party introduced a small earnings-related second tier in 1961, and a more fully developed system was implemented in 1978. While countries such as Canada, Sweden, and Norway simply added a second tier of earnings-related benefits to the state system, Britain introduced a second tier in which employers could contract out of the public system under the condition that they were prepared to provide a benefit package equal or superior to that of the state system. The state, however, assumed the risks involved by providing inflation insurance to meet any unexpected costs of indexing.

Thus, with few exceptions (such as the Netherlands), the flat-rate citizen's *benefit* became the earnings-based citizen's *wage*, a hybrid mixture of citizenship and market-based entitlements. But it did remain a *citizen's* wage. In all countries, the principles of equality and need continued to be an important component of the national benefit systems. Despite the incorporation of market-based inequalities, overall benefit formulas remained redistributive; wage-based formulas continued to provide a higher return on past contributions to low-income groups than to high-income groups.[5] Furthermore, the manner in which the state assumed responsibility for guaranteeing income security through indexing provisions was a clear departure from the risk and uncertainty of the market. As recent controversies over the indexing of private pensions have illustrated, the market is neither willing nor able to provide such protection unless compelled and subsidized by the state (see Pesando and Rea, 1977). Finally, virtually all systems now make adjustments to take need and adequacy into account through such mechanisms as supplementary benefits for additional family dependents, housing benefits, and special pension credits to compensate for years out of the labor force for the purpose of child rearing.

Moreover, as Titmuss anticipated, the abandonment of the flat-benefit system provided a political climate in which the income floor for the poorest among the elderly was raised considerably. An overtly inegalitarian policy had the effect of facilitating the achievement of an egalitarian objective. This is well illustrated by the Canadian reforms of the mid-sixties. The second tier of the Canadian system, the wage-based Canada Pension Plan (CPP), was added to the original flat-benefit system in 1966. But in 1967, a means-tested plan was added (the Guaranteed Income Supplement, or GIS) to provide income to those not covered by CPP and without alternative income sources. By the time these two systems came to maturity, their respective benefit formulas were such that the poorest elderly couple receiving the means-tested Guaranteed Income Supplement was likely to be receiving more than the highest wage-earner was receiving under the earnings-related Canada Pension Plan. In 1978, the maximum monthly benefit under the CPP was $194, whereas the maximum monthly benefit under the GIS formula was $198 for a retired couple. In addition, most provincial governments were providing poor couples with additional benefits of between $202 and $1196 per year. Although the Canadian case is an extreme one, it serves to illustrate Titmuss's point that in a society that is at once democratic and capitalist, policy making is truly a matter of living with contradictions.

Living with Contradictions:
Income Distribution in
the Liberal Democratic State

Commenting on an article entitled "Old Age as a Sociological Problem," published in the *American Journal of Orthopsychiatry* in 1940, Lawrence K. Frank observed: "It may be one of the minor ironies of life that a capitalist society, dedicated to acquisitiveness, is forced to distribute an increasing proportion of the total national income gratuitously, in order to keep running."[6] Frank's perceptiveness in recognizing the contradictions contained in the provision of a citizen's wage in a capitalist economy was marred only by his suggestion that the irony of such a situation is minor. Modern politicians find themselves in the unenviable position of being held responsible for the failures of an economic system they do not control (Lindblom, 1977). As a result, they must create a political climate that maintains "business confidence" (Block, 1977) and avoid policies that discourage those with capital from making the investments necessary to maintain a high level of economic activity. State programs of income distribution that make it possible for individuals and families to maintain a normal standard of living independently of the labor market have always been perceived as a threat to this requirement.

Accordingly, government officials must appear to make every effort to minimize the potential deleterious effects on economic efficiency produced by state systems of income provision. In this respect, the state in all capitalist democracies remains—to a greater or lesser degree—liberal.

The liberal character of modern public pension systems is most clearly manifested in the extent to which income entitlements in old age are tied to previous earnings and other market-based criteria (for example, years in the labor force). By incorporating the rules of the marketplace into its public provisions, the state reminds its citizens that they are not only citizens but also commodities whose value to society is in part determined by the price employers are prepared to pay for their labor. Perhaps less apparent is the historical link between market forces and the flat-benefit system. Where universal flat benefits for the elderly were introduced, benefit levels were typically kept low for two reasons. The first was to ensure that social benefits would not undercut market wages. As Beveridge made clear, his intent was to put a floor under the market, not to replace it. Second (and somewhat ironically), the flat-benefit system found its most avid supporters in the postwar period among the large insurance and trust companies, who recognized that so long as benefits were low, the lucrative and growing private pension market among middle- and upper-income earners would be left untouched. In Canada (Murphy, 1982), Britain (Heclo, 1974), and Denmark (Esping-Andersen, forthcoming), flat benefits provided a compromise between the growing requirement for a universal retirement wage, on the one hand, and business resistance to state encroachment on the growing market for private occupational pensions, on the other hand.

But the modern state is also a democratic state, one in which political representation is based on citizenship and political rights are attached to persons as well as to their property. The principle of "one man, one vote" stands in marked contrast to the principle of "one dollar, one vote" that prevails in the market. As a result, the citizens of the capitalist democracies have been able to establish income claims that are quite independent of market capacity. Throughout the postwar years, claims and entitlements based on criteria of need, adequacy, and equality grew dramatically. Minimum benefits rose to meet demands for adequacy, indexing provisions were adopted to insulate the incomes of the elderly from the inflationary pressures of the marketplace, entitlements for dependents and those outside the labor force were adopted, and general benefit increases were periodically legislated to provide the elderly with a fair share of a growing economic pie. Consequently, the grip of the market over the retirement wage was progressively weakened.

Conclusion

Few classical social theorists would dispute the thrust of the argument so far. The citizen's wage is a reflection of the twin pillars of capitalism and democracy upon which the contemporary welfare state has been constructed. As Flora and Heidenheimer (1981: 22) observe, de Tocqueville, Weber, Marx, and Durkheim would all be equally likely to agree with the conclusion that

> the growth of the modern welfare state can be understood as a response to two fundamental developments: the formation of national states and their transformation into mass democracies after the French Revolution, and the growth of capitalism that became the dominant mode of production after the Industrial Revolution.

But what about the direction of this development? On this issue, there is considerably more disagreement. Some (such as Parsons) have interpreted Marshall's argument as indicating that the expansion of citizenship is an irreversible evolutionary force, slowly carving away the defenses and bastions of classical liberalism (see Goldthorpe, 1978). Others (such as Piven and Cloward, 1971) have argued that advances in social citizenship represent little more than temporary concessions granted by economic and political elites under unusual circumstances, which are then quickly rolled back as stability is restored: in the long run, the principle of class will predominate. But for Marshall, it was clear that the temporary respite in the ongoing war between citizenship and class achieved in the postwar period concealed a chronic underlying tension. He warned: "This phase will not continue indefinitely. It may be that some of the conflicts within our social system are becoming too sharp to achieve its purpose much longer" (Marshall, 1964: 134).

In retrospect, Marshall's foresight appears quite remarkable. By the end of the seventies, cracks were beginning to appear in this historic compromise. In the face of the international economic crisis that began to appear after 1974, the optimism that had characterized the expansionary fifties and sixties began to dissipate, and the view that public welfare and economic efficiency were compatible was increasingly being brought into question (Geiger and Geiger, 1978). The conflict between liberalism and democracy began to rear its head once again. Widespread attention was given to the view that the spread of citizenship entitlements had produced a situation of "democratic overload" that was undermining the economies of the West (Crozier et al., 1975). At the forefront of this debate was the issue of providing increasingly generous benefits to an ever-expanding population of elders (Myles, 1981). As Marshall had predicted, citizenship and social class were once again at war.

Marshall did not speculate on the outcome of this conflict; he wisely recognized that history is a matter of probabilities, not some inexorable law of social change. To establish probabilities is to identify the conditions under which one outcome is more likely to occur than another. Thus, the issue is an empirical one: what conditions favor the further progression of social citizenship, and, by implication, what conditions favor a return to a pure market economy unencumbered by democratic constraints? Here, the past (especially the recent past) can provide us with clues to the future. As they have evolved in the postwar period, the public pension systems of the capitalist democracies have become characterized by varying levels of both citizenship and class entitlements. The mixture of citizenship and social class embodied in pension entitlements is a variable, not a constant. Once we have established this variation empirically (see Chapter 3), it becomes possible to identify the forces that account for it (see Chapter 4). And while the future is never a mirror image of the past, identification of the forces that have advanced the principle of citizenship in the past, combined with an assessment of the current status of those forces, can provide the foundation for predictions about the future.

Notes

1. The story of Bismarck's "invention" of the modern welfare state has been told many times. Perhaps the most useful source is Gaston Rimlinger's *Welfare Policy and Industrialization in Europe, America and Russia* (New York: John Wiley, 1971). Our purpose in this chapter is not to recount the story again but rather to examine the principles of distribution adopted during these early efforts.
2. For a systematic analysis of initial resistance in the United States to European-like social insurance programs, see Skocpol and Ikenberry, 1982.
3. Under Title I of the act, the means-tested Old Age Assistance (OAA) program was also introduced, and during the early years it provided the bulk of state aid to the elderly. As Derthick (1979: 220) observes, left on its own, Congress "would probably have chosen OAA grants and OAA grants only." Title II (old-age insurance) was introduced at the insistence of the executive branch and eventually became the core of the program now identified in the United States as Social Security.
4. An early comparison of the systems in the United States and Canada was conducted by Robert M. Clark for the Canadian government. See Robert M. Clark, *Economic Security for the Aged in the United States and Canada:*

A Report Prepared for the Government of Canada (Ottawa: Queen's Printer, 1960).

5. For a description of how this is achieved in the United States, see Derthick (1979: 256).

6. I am grateful to William Graebner for drawing this quotation to my attention.

Chapter

3

The Citizen's Wage in Comparative Perspective

The search for a set of principles to guide the distributional practices of the liberal democratic state may be broadly construed as a process of convergence. Where initial legislation was designed to reflect strict rules of market equity, the laws were subsequently modified to meet democratic demands that the state also recognize differences in individual need, ensure a modicum of security, and provide minimum levels of income adequacy. Benefit levels originally intended to put a floor under the market were subsequently raised to supplement and replace it. Conversely, strict adherence to egalitarianism in the political sphere proved to be generally incompatible with the inegalitarian forces of a market economy. As a result, all national systems came to reflect the twin pillars of citizenship and social class. But convergence in principle is not convergence in practice. While policy makers in all liberal democratic states are faced with similar constraints, they do not respond to those constraints in identical fashion. Consequently, there is considerable variation in the value and composition of the citizen's wage across countries, the result of differences in the level and structure of benefits and in the guidelines that regulate accessibility to these benefits.

The purpose of this chapter is to examine the citizen's wage in practice. In the first part of the chapter, the major elements that enter the design of any public pension system are identified. These elements are at once the building blocks of public pension policy and critical points at which policy makers must decide on the mixture of distributional criteria to be incorporated into the system. The exposition is illustrated with comparisons of the public pension systems of Canada, Sweden, and the United States.[1] In the sections that follow, the scope of the analysis is broadened in order to develop a composite index of the quality of public pensions in fifteen capitalist democracies. The index of pension quality, in turn, provides the basis of the analysis to follow in Chapter 4.

The Aged, the State, and the Structure of Inequality

In a market economy, the position of most individuals in the distribution of income is determined by the attributes and skills they bring to the labor market, where they compete for positions to which different rewards are attached. During the preretirement years, a structure of income inequality emerges that reflects this reward hierarchy. As each cohort makes the transition into retirement, the preretirement distribution of income is transformed. Typically, income levels decline relative to both preretirement income levels and the standard of living in the larger society. Individuals within a cohort may also change place in the ordering of rich and poor, the result of differential accumulation of retirement-income entitlements. And, finally, the level of inequality within a cohort may either increase or decline. The public pension systems of the capitalist democracies may be usefully thought of as the aggregate of policies designed to affect this transformation. Public officials may choose to leave the preretirement income structure more or less intact or to alter it in accordance with other nonmarket criteria of allocation.

The choices confronting policy makers in this regard may be usefully divided into choices concerning the level of benefits and choices concerning the structure of benefits. *Level* refers to the value of the pension benefit relative to previous earnings or to the standard of living in the larger society. *Structure* refers to the degree of gradation in the distribution of benefits. An ungraduated, flat-benefit system will provide the same pension to all, irrespective of past earnings and contributions. The more closely benefits are linked to earnings and contributions, the more graduated the system will be.

In designing a pension system, the state is faced with the difficult problem of determining how much inequality it will tolerate both within the elderly population and between the elderly population and the larger society. The more the benefit structure departs from the flat-benefit principle (that is, the more graduated it becomes), the greater the income inequality will be within the elderly population. In addition, policy makers must attend to the level of benefits if they are to prevent the elderly from becoming a negatively privileged group at the bottom of the societal income hierarchy. Regardless of the structure of the system, the elderly will be poor if the average benefit

Table 3.1
Replacement Ratios and the Structure of Inequality

Properties of the distribution of replacement ratios		Structure of inequality	
Benefit level	Benefit structure	Intergenerational inequality	Intragenerational inequality
High	Flat	Low	Low
Low	Flat	High	Low
High	Graduated	Low	High
Low	Graduated	High	High

Source: Adapted from John F. Myles, "The Aged, the State and the Structure of Inequality." In J. Harp and J. Hofley (eds.), *Structured Inequality in Canada* (Scarborough: Prentice-Hall of Canada, 1980). By permission of Prentice-Hall of Canada, Inc.

level is low relative to the standard of living in the society as a whole.

The implications of these two dimensions of any pension system—structure and level—are summarized in Table 3.1. Each row of Table 3.1 may be considered as representing one of four hypothetical systems. A flat-benefit system with high benefit levels will produce a population of elders among whom there is little inequality and whose standard of living approximates that of the society as a whole. In contrast, a flat-benefit system with low benefit levels will produce an elderly population that is equal but poor in relation to the larger society. The third system—high benefit levels and a graduated structure—will result in considerable inequality within the elderly population, but with the elderly no more likely than the non-elderly to be poor. Finally, low benefit levels and a graduated system will produce considerable inequality both within the elderly population and between the elderly and the non-elderly. Such pure types, of course, do not exist anywhere today. Rather, these two dimensions of national pension systems provide us with a set of variables (structure and level) to guide our investigation of the citizen's wage.

Policy makers rarely make decisions about the structure of inequality per se. Instead, choices tend to be guided by the broader principles of distribution discussed in Chapter 2—principles of security, adequacy, and need. The concept of *income security* connotes the idea of a level of income that allows individuals to maintain preretirement living standards throughout the retirement years. To measure income security, policy analysts typically employ a measure called the *replacement ratio*. The numerator of the replacement ratio is the annual total value of all public pensions received after retirement; the denominator is the level of annual earnings just prior to retirement. Thus, an employee with a salary of $20,000 per year who retires on a pension of $10,000 per year would have an income replacement ratio of 0.50. Economists generally agree that if one is to maintain one's preretirement living standard, retirement income must replace between 60 and 80 percent of preretirement earnings.

The criterion of income security can be perfectly satisfied by a benefit structure that exactly mirrors the earnings distribution prior to retirement. Thus, with respect to structure, the security principle does not require violation of market principles of distribution. But the same is not true with respect to the level of benefits. If total lifetime contributions plus accrued interest (imputed or real) fall below the level necessary to produce the required income flows, provision of income security to the elderly will require transfers from the working to the retired population. Historically, such transfers have been required in virtually all old-age pension schemes (Rosa, 1982). Moreover, to provide income security through the public sector requires that a choice be made to exclude the private sector from the pension field because the demand for private pensions is effectively eliminated. As a result, state efforts to satisfy the security principle have typically had to overcome (or have been frustrated by) the resistance of those market actors for whom the private pension market represents a major source of business activity (insurance and trust companies). And in recent years, these traditional opponents of public-sector pensions have been joined by the much larger set of industrial firms for whom private pension funds have become a major source of new investment capital (Myles, 1980; Murphy, 1982).

For individuals at the bottom of the income hierarchy, income security is not a very comforting concept, since it in no way assures *income adequacy*. To provide income security to the poor is only to secure them in their poverty. The concept of income adequacy rests on political and moral judgments and thus is subject to considerable variation. It has most typically been evaluated in relationship to conventionally understood definitions of poverty (the minimum income required for survival). Increasingly, however, it has come to reflect a more democratic view of equality, according to which all citizens ought to receive a share of the social product sufficient to permit a standard of living comparable to that of society as a whole (Geiger and Geiger, 1978: 10). For this objective of adequacy to be achieved, income replacement ratios for low-income earners must be considerably higher than those for high-income earners.

A third principle of distribution incorporated into most contemporary public pension schemes is that of need. This is sometimes confounded with adequacy, but the two are best kept distinct as concepts. Whereas the principle of adequacy usually requires vertical redistribution from high-income groups to low-income groups, the criterion of need may also require horizontal transfers within income groups (for example, from those with small families to those with large families, from those without handicaps to those with handicaps, etc.). Both criteria, of course, are intended to enhance equality of condition, and both violate the market-based rule of equity, which is satisfied only when benefits are proportional to contributions. Strict application of the equity rule requires that all entitlements be "purchased" with contributions plus real or imputed interest. Benefits may then be considered a form of property rather than entitlements of citizenship.

To illustrate these concepts, we can consult Table 3.2, which provides income replacement ratios for low-, medium-, and high-

Table 3.2
Income Replacement Ratios for Low-, Medium-, and High-Income Earners in Canada, the United States, and Sweden

| | Earnings level before retirement | | |
	Half average earnings	Average earnings	Twice average earnings
A: One-Earner Couples			
Canada			
(a) With guaranteed income supplement	101	54	—
(b) Without guaranteed income supplement	78	46	23
Sweden	110	80	54
United States	82	61	35
B: Single Earners and Two-Earner Couples			
Canada			
(a) With guaranteed income supplement	59	33	—
(b) Without guaranteed income supplement	52	30	15
Sweden	70	60	43
United States	56	41	22

Source: Estimates are derived from Hart D. Clark, "A Comparison of the Retirement Income Systems of Canada and Other Countries." In *Canadian Government Task Force on Retirement Policy* (Hull, Quebec: Canadian Government Publishing Centre, 1980).

income earners in Canada, the United States, and Sweden. Of these three, Sweden comes closest to satisfying all three principles of distribution. Its high replacement ratios at the middle- and upper-income levels ensure a high level of income security for all elderly Swedes. In contrast, upper- and middle-income earners in the United States and Canada experience a significant drop in living standards in old age unless public benefits are supplemented by private pensions and personal savings.

The principle of adequacy is reflected in the inverse relationship between previous earnings and the size of the replacement ratio. In the United States, this is the result of a Social Security benefit formula that favors low-income earners. In Sweden and Canada, the higher replacement ratios of low-income earners reflect the first tier of universal flat-benefit pensions paid to all citizens regardless of work history or previous contributions. Canada's Guaranteed Income Supplement provides additional means-tested benefits for those without alternative sources of income. And in Sweden, additional pension entitlements are provided to those who have accumulated few or no credits under the earnings-related pension system (ATP).

The principle of need is reflected in the adjustments made by all three systems for the one-earner couple. These adjustments are shown in the differences between sections A and B of Table 3.2. In the United States, a retiring worker with a dependent spouse (one who has not accumulated Social Security credits) receives a supplement equal to 50 percent of the basic benefit. In Canada and Sweden, this adjustment takes the form of the additional flat-benefit pension going to each household, plus adjustments made through supplementary credit programs. The joint effects of these supplementary benefits for low-income earners with dependent spouses are quite pronounced in Canada and Sweden. Low-income earners in both countries are slightly better off after retirement than before retirement. At the middle-income levels, adjustments for a dependent spouse are approximately the same in all three countries, whereas for upper-income earners, the largest adjustment is made in the United States.

While the structure and the level of replacement ratios are the basic building blocks of any public pension system, they are by no means the only components that determine the level of economic well-being of the elderly. Two additional factors must be considered before we reach conclusions about the relative quality of various national pension systems—the stability of these ratios over time (the problem of indexing) and the relative ease with which the elderly members of a nation can gain access to the public system.

The Stability of Replacement Ratios:
The Problem of Indexing

Replacement ratios are indicative of how well elderly individuals and couples can expect to fare during the first year of retirement, but the ratios do not describe what will happen in subsequent years. If benefit levels are not adjusted to reflect inflation (price increases), the real value of these replacement ratios will deteriorate very quickly. The purchasing power of the pension benefit will be eroded, and in a few years a high initial replacement ratio will be worth very little.

But even adjustments for inflation will not prevent the elderly from falling to the bottom of the national income distribution in a society where the real standard of living is rising—that is, where wages are increasing faster than prices. Pension benefits that reflect wage levels of a decade or two ago are very low by today's standards. Consequently, an elderly person who retired on a "good" pension in the early sixties may be quite poor by current standards of living despite price indexing. Recognition of this fact has led some countries to link benefit increases to wages rather than to prices. Other nations have adopted a combination of the two criteria, usually adjusting benefits on the basis of which of the two—prices or wages—increases the most (see Table 3.3). With wage indexing, the fate of the elderly is tied to the fate of the economy as a whole; the elderly benefit from real growth in the economy but share the losses produced by a falling standard of living. With price indexing, the individual's real standard of living is preserved over time, but he or she does not share in the wealth produced by real economic growth or the losses produced by downturns in the economy.

It is not only the means of indexing that is important, but also the frequency with which it is done. Canada, the United States, and the United Kingdom adjust benefits annually. France and the Netherlands make adjustments twice a year. Sweden has one of the most responsive systems, raising benefits whenever there is a 3 percent change in the consumer price index sustained for two months. The more frequent the indexing, the higher the lifetime income of the elderly individual. Actual increases in pensions, of course, reflect not only indexing provision but also periodic legislative changes that raise benefits for all.

Table 3.4 shows the pattern of growth in pension benefits for eight countries during the period from 1960 to 1973. An index value less than one indicates that pensions rose more slowly than wages or prices, and a value greater than one indicates that pensions rose faster than wages or prices. Throughout the period, benefits rose considerably faster than prices in all countries. The majority raised

Table 3.3
Pension Indexing in Selected Countries

Indexing by prices	Indexing by wages	Combination of wages and prices
Canada	France	Finland
Japan	The Netherlands	Italy
Sweden	West Germany	Switzerland
United States		United Kingdom

Source: Barbara Torrey and Carole Thompson, *An International Comparison of Pension Systems*, President's Commission on Pension Policy (Washington: Government Printing Office, 1980), p. 18.

benefits in line with wages, providing the elderly with a share of the real economic growth that occurred. Until recently, wage indexing was considered to be more advantageous for the elderly because wages typically rose faster than prices. Since the mid-seventies, however, when real wages began to decline and prices continued to rise, price indexing has generally been more advantageous to the elderly, narrowing income differentials between old and young.

The issue of indexing is most closely linked to the principle of income security. When the real value of an individual's savings or assets is eroded by inflation, the value lost simply seems to disappear because no direct transfer has occurred. But in fact such wealth is

Table 3.4
Changes in Pensions Relative to Wages and Prices in Eight Industrialized Countries, 1960–1974

	Pensions/wages	Pensions/prices
Canada[a]	0.90	1.21
Sweden[b]	0.98	1.43
United States	1.04	1.22
United Kingdom	1.29	2.92
Germany	0.94	1.80
France	1.09	1.86
Switzerland	2.09	3.43

[a]Excludes earnings-related pensions.
[b]Period is 1960–1973.
Source: Hart D. Clark, "A Comparison of the Retirement Income Systems of Canada and Other Countries." In *Canadian Government Task Force on Retirement Policy* (Hull, Quebec: Canadian Government Publishing Centre, 1980). Reproduced by permission of the Ministre of Supply and Services Canada.

simply redistributed, usually from lenders to borrowers. Thus, in the private pension markets of Canada and the United States, inflation has tended to transfer wealth from employees and pensioners to employers and the issuers of fixed-income securities (Pesando and Rea, 1977). Price indexing removes the insecurity produced by unanticipated inflation and prevents the wealth transfers that would otherwise take place. In contrast, wage indexing may be more appropriately thought of as a form of solidarity between active and retired workers. Pensioners are provided with a share of the new wealth created in periods of economic growth but, in turn, are required to suffer the setbacks produced when the economy flounders. Historically, however, both forms of indexing have represented positive interventions by the state to insulate the incomes of the elderly from the distributive and redistributive effects of the marketplace.

Access to Pensions: The Problem of Eligibility

The level, structure, and stability of replacement ratios constitute the core of any public pension system. But national pension systems also vary considerably in the degree to which these benefits are made accessible to citizens. In some nations, all or part of the benefits available through the public pension system are available on the basis of a single criterion—citizenship. But most countries use more or less stringent labor-market criteria to assess eligibility for full benefits. For those individuals who do not meet these criteria, full benefits will not be forthcoming.

As we have seen, Canada and Sweden provide a universal flat-benefit pension to all citizens (and to noncitizens meeting certain residency requirements) who have reached the age of 65. These are citizenship entitlements paid to the elderly irrespective of labor-market criteria. In addition, Sweden provides supplementary benefits for those not covered by the national earnings-based system (ATP). These suppplementary benefits are not means-tested and are extended whether or not the individual has other sources of income. The United States has no comparable guaranteed citizen's benefit available to all.

Both Canada and the United States, however, do provide minimum income-tested benefits. These are entitlements of citizenship, but they are available only to those lacking alternative sources of income. This benefit is provided in Canada through the Guaranteed Income Supplement, introduced in 1967, and in the United States through Supplementary Security Income (SSI), introduced in 1974.

In 1978, a married couple could receive up to $284 in the United States under SSI and $198 in Canada under GIS. But the Canadian supplement was in addition to the universal benefit under Old Age Security, so the Canadian system provided a guaranteed minimum of $6190 per year to a married couple, as compared with a guaranteed minimum of $3408 per year in the United States.

Eligibility criteria for full benefits under earnings-related systems also vary considerably. Full benefits require 40 years of covered earnings under the Canada Pension Plan, 39 years of covered earnings under U.S. Social Security, and 30 years of covered earnings under the Swedish ATP. Thus, workers who have had interrupted work histories and shorter periods in the labor force are more likely to be eligible for full benefits in Sweden than in either Canada or the United States. Eligibility for minimum benefits in the United States is also subject to labor-market restrictions. To be eligible for Social Security in 1979, for example, workers retiring at age 62 needed 28 quarters (or approximately seven years) of coverage, with the requirement rising one quarter in each succeeding year. Canada and Sweden do not have a retirement test (individuals receive benefits whether or not they continue to work), whereas U.S. Social Security benefits are reduced in proportion to earned income until age 72. Both Sweden and the United States allow for early retirement at reduced benefit levels; Canada has no such provision. All of these factors raise or decrease the probability of an individual's gaining access to the full benefits provided under the public pension system. The more stringent the criteria, the less likely it is that the system will satisfy the principles of security, adequacy, and need.

From Principle to Practice: Citizenship and Social Class in Canada, Sweden, and the United States

Despite the apparent differences in these three systems, it is clear that they have been guided in their development by similar criteria of distribution. As indicated by the structure of replacement ratios, all three systems continue to mirror the wage-based inequalities of the market. And in Canada, where the link to previous earnings is weakest, benefit levels for the average worker have been kept low. Consequently, Canadians, more than Americans or Swedes, must rely on market-based entitlements (private pensions and savings) to maintain their standard of living in old age. But it is also apparent that market entitlements in all three systems have been modified to satisfy criteria of security, adequacy, and need. To provide *income security* to the elderly, administrators have found it necessary to provide benefit levels considerably higher than those that the average worker could acquire through personal savings or the private pension market.[2] to ensure *income adequacy*, all three countries provide for some redistribution from high-income to low-income earners. And to meet the needs of families with different consumption requirements, all three nations redistribute income from two-earner couples and single individuals to single-earner couples.

These similarities at the level of principle, however, only serve to highlight the varying approaches to the appropriate relationship between state and economy that are evident in practice. The Swedish public pension system is largely the creation of the Social Democratic Party, which held power continuously from the 1930s to the mid-seventies. The long-term objective of the Social Democrats was to make the market irrelevant in the distributional process. In attempting to do so, however, they faced a dilemma. Gearing public entitlements to the wage inequalities of the market would reproduce the stratifying effects of class that the policy makers sought to overcome. Failure to follow market practices, on the other hand, would reduce the commitment of middle- and upper-income earners to the public sector, encourage the expansion of private sector plans, and limit efforts to raise benefits for those at the bottom of the wage hierarchy. Thus, the pursuit of citizenship had to be tempered by the realities of class. The Social Democrats' solution to this dilemma was to create a generous welfare state for all wage-earners as well as to pursue greater equality through labor-market policies designed to reduce wage differentials in the marketplace.

In contrast, the U.S. Social Security system continues to reflect the neoliberal objectives of its founders. The rugged individualism of traditional laissez-faire liberalism was abandoned in favor of an interventionist state, but only to the extent necessary to save the market from destruction. The objective, as Esping-Andersen (1982: 11) observes, was to provide the means to ensure that "individual self-reliance could actually work." Old-age security was to conform to the principles of social insurance under which "risks are socialized while the individual retains the lion's share of responsibility in the form of contribution and work effort" (Esping-Andersen, 1982: 11). Whereas in Sweden and Canada the entitlements of low-income earners are citizenship entitlements that are independent of previous earnings and work effort, U.S. citizens who have not earned sufficient Social Security credits must rely on the much lower benefits provided under Supplemental Security Income. Compared to the Swedish system, U.S. Social Security is also distinguished by the room it leaves for private sector initiatives.

The dominant feature of the Canadian system is the degree to which it continues to approximate the flat-benefit approach of Lord Beveridge. While the safety net for the elderly is more secure in Canada than in the United States, middle- and upper-income Canadians receive minimal income protection from the public sector. Consequently, they are even more dependent on the private pension market and personal savings than are their counterparts in the United States. Clearly, such variation calls for explanation. Such explanation, however, requires both a more precise codification of these differences and a broadening of the scope of the analysis. It is to these tasks that we turn next.

An Index of the Citizen's Wage

As the preceding discussion illustrates, arriving at measures of cross-national differences in the quality of public pensions is a complex task. Indeed, some researchers have concluded that it is impossible and have fallen back on "subjective" rankings of the quality and character of different national systems (see Kaim-Caudle, 1973: 300). First, it is necessary to specify precisely what is to be compared. Is the object to compare pension systems or income-maintenance systems for the elderly? The two are by no means identical. Consider Table 3.5, where the disbursements made to the

Table 3.5
Expenditures on Goods and Services
for the Elderly as a Percentage of
Total Expenditures on the Elderly,
European Economic Community
Countries, 1974

	Percent
Belgium	0.5
Denmark	26.4
Germany	0.8
France	n.a.
Ireland	9.9
Italy	0.5
The Netherlands	1.9
United Kingdom	4.3

Source: Statistical Office of the European Communities, *Social Accounts: 1970–75* (Brussels: European Economic Community, 1977), Table 31.

elderly in the form of goods and services (in-kind benefits) in the countries of the European Economic Community (EEC) are expressed as a percentage of all disbursements made to the elderly. The omission of expenditures on goods and services would alter the picture very little for five of the six countries but would alter the picture dramatically for Denmark, which provides over a quarter of its support for the elderly in this way.

Countries may also allocate income to the elderly through tax expenditures. Rather than increasing the size of the monthly pension check, the government may simply allow the elderly to retain a higher pecentage of that check by taxing benefits at a lower rate than other income or by taxing the total income of the elderly at a lower rate than that applied to the younger population. A study conducted by the Union of Swiss Banks (1977) found that income-replacement ratios before taxes for an average retired couple were virtually identical in Canada and the Netherlands—53.1 percent in Canada and 55.5 percent in the Netherlands. After taxes, however, the real income-replacement ratios were 80.4 percent in the Netherlands and 62.1 percent in Canada.

A further difficulty arises when one attempts to distinguish between what is private and what is public. Most comparative studies of public policy direct their attention to public sector pensions, since it is public policy (what is done by the state) that is under consideration. But the two are not always easy to distinguish. Should occupational pensions for state employees be included in the public sector? The expenditure data routinely published by the International Labor Organization (ILO) include pensions for state employees, whereas the accounts of the Organization for Economic Cooperation and Development (OECD, 1976) do not. Such pensions, it is argued, are similar to occupational plans in the private sector and, hence, should be excluded when the purpose is to determine how well the state provides for the elderly in their capacity as citizens. Cross-national variations in expenditures that include pensions for state employees may simply be measuring differences in the relative economic well-being of retired government workers.

Equally troublesome is the existence of mandated pensions in some countries. Rather than increase state pensions, several countries have addressed the problem of providing old-age security by means of laws requiring employers to participate in pension schemes that are not state administered and do not appear in the government accounts. Nonetheless, such programs should be considered policy outputs, an effect of the political system on the economic well-being of the elderly. France has such a system, and similar proposals are under consideration in Switzerland and the Netherlands. In Japan and the

United Kingdom, employers may opt out of the public system if they provide a pension equivalent to that provided by the public system. Finally, private sector pensions typically receive enormous subsidies from the state in the form of tax concessions on contributions. Thus, a significant portion of private sector benefits should be included under public sector expenditures.

A second issue concerns the type of data to be used. Cross-national comparisons of welfare-state development typically make use of two different data sources—public expenditure data and policy data. The former, based on national accounts, include all expenditures made on welfare in general (Wilensky, 1975) or on certain programs such as pensions (see Chapter 1). Expenditures are first standardized to reflect national differences in the standard of living and then averaged across beneficiaries to produce a figure that measures the typical or average benefit received. Although we shall have occasion to make use of such data, they suffer from several major defects. First, average benefit levels say nothing about the manner in which benefits are distributed. Average benefit levels may be higher in one country than in another but disproportionately allocated to those with large incomes from other sources. An example is shown in Table 3.6. The first column of this table presents an index value called the transfer ratio.[3] It is computed by dividing the average pension benefit by the Gross Domestic Product (GDP) per capita and may be construed as a rough index of the generosity of the pension system. The second column indicates the share of total pension benefits received by the bottom income quintile in each country. The figures indicate that Germany and France spend more per capita on

Table 3.6
Index of Pension "Generosity" and Share of Bottom Income Quintile in Public Pension Benefits for Five Countries, 1972 or Near Date

	Transfer ratio	Share of bottom quintile in total pensions
Belgium	.441	6.9%
France	.521	4.7%
Germany	.655	6.7%
Italy	.345	11.5%
United Kingdom	.299	13.2%

Source: Organization for Economic Cooperation and Development, "Public Expenditure on Income Maintenance Programmes" (Paris: OECD, 1976), p. 24.

pensions but that less of the money is directed toward those at the bottom of the income distribution.

Further, public expenditure data do not take into account important differences in the social composition of the population of beneficiaries. Identical types of individuals may be receiving identical benefits in two countries, but because of variation in the age, sex, and marital status of the beneficiaries, overall expenditures and average benefit levels may differ dramatically. Although such data are satisfactory to measure the volume of expenditures, they are of limited use in assessing the content of the policies that generate these expenditures.

Because of these difficulties, comparative studies of pension policy have increasingly come to rely on the policies themselves as a source of data—replacement ratios, indexing provisions, and eligibility criteria (Day, 1978; Maguire, 1981; Esping-Andersen, 1981). To construct a composite index of public pension quality, analysts first rank-order countries on each component. A system of weights reflecting the theoretical construct being measured is then assigned to the components, and the weighted scores are added together to provide a single value for each country. A similar procedure is followed here.

The index of the citizen's wage, developed in the following pages, relies principally on the work of Day (1978), which is to date the most comprehensive effort to measure cross-national differences in public pension systems. Day's analysis provides index values for 15 capitalist democracies in 1975. These values have been modified in two ways for the present analysis. First, the scalar values assigned by Day were checked against other comparative data sources (Esping-Andersen, 1981; Haanes-Olsen, 1978; Canadian Task Force on Retirement Policy, 1979; Organization for Economic Cooperation and Development, 1977) as well as against country-specific sources, and adjustments were made where indicated. The criteria for assigning scalar values to each component are presented in the Appendix to this chapter. Second, the weighting system developed by Day was altered to reflect the theoretical focus of the present analysis. The components and criteria for weighting are discussed below.

The Structure and Level of Benefits

Benefit levels for low-, average-, and high-income earners are measured as a proportion of the average male wage in non-agricultural occupations; these relative benefit levels identify the degree of income security provided by the system.[4] Adjustments are made for the supplements provided for a dependent spouse, in order to reflect the degree to which the system satisfies need. Adequacy is measured by assigning weights that are inversely proportional to preretirement income levels. In effect, policy characteristics that benefit low-income earners are weighted more heavily than those that benefit high-income earners. This conforms to conventional notions of economic welfare defined in terms of declining marginal utility: an additional dollar of income is assumed to increase the welfare of a poor person more than that of a rich person. The general result of this procedure is to assign higher scores to those systems that come closest to satisfying simultaneously the criteria of security, adequacy, and need. The components and their associated weights are as follows:

Component	Weight
1. Maximum pension available to the lowest-paid worker (and dependent spouse) as a percentage of the average male wage in nonagriculture.	4
2. Maximum pension available to the worker (and dependent spouse) whose average wage has been equal to the average male wage in non-agriculture as a percentage of the average male wage in non-agriculture.	3
3. Maximum pension available to the highest-paid worker (and dependent spouse) as a percentage of the average male wage in non-agriculture.	2

Stability and Accessibility

The stability of replacement ratios over time (indexing) and ease of accessibility to pension entitlements are measured with the following indicators:

Component	Weight
4. Frequency and degree of cost-of-living adjustments.	4
5. Degree of means testing.	3
6. Universality of coverage.	1
7. Degree of flexibility in age at which one qualifies for pension.	2
8. Degree of retirement required to qualify.	1

Item 4 (indexing) is more heavily weighted than Items 5 through 8 because it is the only indicator of the stability of benefit levels included in the scale. The remaining indicators all measure the relative ease of accessibility to the public pension system and, in particular, the degree to which accessibility is independent of previous labor-force participation. Item 5 is more heavily weighted, since it is probably the most reliable estimate of the extent of pension coverage. The highest scores (values 8–10) on this indicator are given to countries that have a universal pension available to all citizens, the next highest to countries that combine an employment-based public system with a means-tested system, and the lowest score to those countries where no guaranteed minimum is assured. Item 6 (universality of coverage) is given a lower weight because it is more prone to measurement error and is somewhat redundant when combined with Item 5. Item 7 is more heavily weighted than Item 8, since provisions for early retirement are more likely to benefit low-income earners whereas the imposition of a retirement test is more likely to penalize high-income earners.[5]

The results for the 15 capitalist democracies included in Day's analysis for 1975 are presented in Table 3.7. Columns one through eight correspond to the eight dimensions defined above. The values in these columns are computed by multiplying the scalar value of each item (see the Appendix to this chapter) by its corresponding weight. For example, on Item 1, Australia has a scalar value of 6, which is then multiplied by 4 to produce a weighted grade of 24. The ninth column gives the total composite score for each country, and the tenth column provides the original composite scores computed by Day. Despite the adjustments made, there is a high degree of consistency between the two sets of scores. The major changes brought about by these adjustments are the lower scores of Austria, Denmark, West Germany, New Zealand, Switzerland, and the United Kingdom.

To assess the validity of the index, we can determine how well it correlates with other measures and indicators of pension quality. Expenditure data are unsatisfactory as measures of pension quality because they tell us nothing about how expenditures are distributed or to whom. Nonetheless, given the nature of the index, it should yield moderate to high correlations with expenditure-based measures, since more generous benefits and more adequate coverage ought to lead to higher overall levels of expenditure on the elderly. Accordingly, correlations between the index of pension quality and a variety of expenditure-based measures available from the OECD publication, *Public Expenditure on Income Maintenance Programmes* (1976) were estimated. The OECD study includes all countries in our sample except Switzerland. Because of this omission, Stephens's (1979) expenditure-based measure of welfare-state effort, which covers all 15 countries, is also included.

The correlations of the index of pension quality with total social

Table 3.7
Weighted Grades on Eight Dimensions of Pension Policy in 15 Capitalist Democracies, 1975

	1	2	3	4	5	6	7	8	Total	Day
Australia	24	12	6	4	15	8	8	2	79	77
Austria	24	21	20	32	15	7	20	6	145	160
Belgium	16	18	10	36	15	7	20	2	124	121
Canada	28	15	8	32	27	10	4	10	134	130
Denmark	28	15	8	36	27	10	10	10	144	167
Finland	28	21	20	40	27	10	14	8	168	167
France	20	15	12	36	15	7	16	8	131	140
The Netherlands	32	15	10	40	24	10	6	10	147	150
New Zealand	24	12	14	36	24	10	6	10	136	158
Norway	28	18	20	40	30	10	4	8	158	159
Sweden	36	24	20	40	30	10	16	10	186	174
Switzerland	24	15	12	24	15	10	8	10	118	142
United Kingdom	20	12	6	28	24	10	8	3	111	130
United States	24	18	12	32	15	6	14	3	120	115
West Germany	16	15	10	28	15	7	14	10	115	156
Average	24.8	16.4	12.5	32.3	21.2	8.8	11.2	7.5	134.4	143.0
Weight	4	3	2	4	3	1	2	1		

security benefit expenditures (standardized on GDP per capita) and with Stephen's measure of welfare-state effort are .57 and .67, respectively. Thus, the index correlates rather well with these global measures of welfare-state development. These measures, however, include all public income-maintenance expenditures. A direct measure of the relative generosity of public pensions per se is the average per capita pension benefit divided by average earnings (OECD, 1978: 23). Although it is in the expected direction, the correlation of this item with the index of pension quality is only .22. Inspection of a scatterplot diagram, however, indicates that this low correlation is a function of two outliers—Germany and France, the two highest-scored countries on the expenditure-based measure. When these two countries are excluded, the correlation rises to a very significant .74. But why do we have the two outliers? Inspection of the OECD data suggests that the error lies more in the OECD estimates of pension expenditures than in the index values. In computing average benefits for Germany and France, OECD officials had to impute estimates because several vital pieces of information were missing (OECD, 1978: 21). Moreover, pension expenditures should be a reasonably good predictor of overall social security expenditures, which they are, but only after Germany and France are excluded from the analysis.

The most salient piece of evidence on this point is the correlation between the index of pension quality and the OECD (1978: 39) measure of real change in average pension benefit levels over the ten-year period from 1962 to 1972 ($r = .73$), with Germany and France included. Cross-sectional estimates are subject to measurement error arising from differences in national accounting systems (that is, from the use of different measurement instruments). Change scores are unaffected by this bias because they are measured with the same instrument. The high correlation between the index of pension quality and changes in real benefit levels for this ten-year period gives further support to our assessment of the OECD figures for Germany and France. While the constructed index is no doubt subject to measurement error, this assessment of its external validity does indicate that it measures what it purports to measure.

It is important, nonetheless, to bear in mind that what is being measured is the public pension system narrowly defined and not the entire range of income-assistance programs available to the elderly. To the extent that other forms of assistance (in-kind transfers, tax assistance, etc.) are administered as functional equivalents to (or substitutes for) the public pension system, the index of pension quality will be biased in favor of those countries that rely more heavily on pensions as a form of income maintenance. The high correlations between the index and the global measures of welfare-state effort, however, suggest that those nations with a generous pension system also tend to be more generous in their other public programs.

Conclusion

With the appearance of an incipient world recession in the middle of the 1970s, three decades of postwar reconstruction and welfare reform came to a standstill. The mid-seventies, then, provides an appropriate point for taking stock of the gains in citizenship entitlements made during this period. Although the trend toward improved entitlements for the elderly was universal, the outcome was by no means uniform. As indicated in Table 3.8, the old-age entitlements in the capitalist democracies ranged from the highly developed public pension system of Sweden to the modest means-tested benefits available to elderly Australians. The Nordic countries and several of the smaller Western European nations (Austria, the Netherlands) were clustered at the high end of the continuum; the larger Western European and North American countries were distributed throughout the lower and intermediate ranges. Ironically, the United Kingdom, a country that came to be synonymous with the welfare state in the postwar years, was among the outstanding laggards in the area of pension reform.[6]

But from whence do these differences spring? Since all of these countries are characterized by a highly developed set of formally democratic political institutions, it is plausible to assume that differences in public policy reflect national differences in the preferences of the electorate: some national cultures simply place a greater value on supporting the elderly than do others. But despite demo-

Table 3.8
The Quality of the Citizen's Wage in 15 Capitalist Democracies, 1975

160 +	Sweden, Finland
150–159	Norway
140–149	The Netherlands, Austria, Denmark
130–139	New Zealand, Canada, France
120–129	Belgium, United States
110–119	Switzerland, United Kingdom, West Germany
Less than 110	Australia

cracy, only rarely do we find that government policy is the mirror image of voter preferences. Were it a mirror image, we would expect to find little variation in the quality of old-age entitlements in the capitalist democracies, for, as Coughlin (1979: 16) has shown, popular demand for generous state pensions for the elderly is uniformly high and shows little variation across countries. This is not to say that values and culture are irrelevant to the policy process, and Achenbaum (1983: 12) is undoubtedly correct in his assertion that the evolution of old-age policies represents "new resolutions to enduring value dilemmas." All public policy makers have been forced to choose between equity and adequacy, between self-reliance and social solidarity, and, more generally, between the principles of liberalism and those of democracy. But to state that variations in policy choices reflect variations in values does not identify the forces that determine the direction in which value dilemmas tend to be resolved. The origins of these value dilemmas, I have argued, are to be found in the structural contradictions inherent in the conjunction of a democratic polity and a capitalist economy. The task that remains is to determine the forces that have led policy makers in the capitalist democracies to resolve these dilemmas in different ways.

Notes

1. A more detailed description of these three systems may be found in Schulz et al. (1974).
2. Schulz (1980: 78) estimates that an annual savings rate of 20 percent of earnings over the entire work life would be necessary to ensure a 60–65 percent replacement ratio on retirement, a figure that is clearly unattainable except for those at the top of the income hierarchy.
3. Data are from the Organization for Economic Cooperation and Development, 1976. Inspection of the source material used for these estimates suggests that these figures overestimate the values of the transfer ratio for Germany and France. They are adequate for their illustrative purpose, however.
4. As in the work of Day (1978), relative benefit levels are used rather than the more conventional replacement ratios. The latter, however, are simple mathematical transformations of the former.
5. The tendency to take early retirement is higher among the more arduous working-class occupations; the tendency to postpone retirement until a more advanced age is higher among upper-middle-class professional and managerial groups.
6. Subsequent improvements in the earnings-related portion of the British system were introduced in 1978. They will not come to full maturity, however, until 1998.

Appendix: Scaling Procedure Used in the Construction of the Index of Pension Quality for 15 Countries, 1975

The procedures used to construct scale values for each of the eight items included in the index of pension quality are adapted from Day (1978). Items for which the scaling procedure was significantly altered from that used by Day are indicated by an asterisk.

1. Maximum pension available to the lowest-paid workers (and dependent spouse) as a percentage of the average male wage in non-agriculture.

Grade	Criterion	Grade	Criterion
10	72+	5	32–39
9	64–71	4	24–31
8	56–63	3	16–23
7	48–55	2	8–15
6	40–47	1	0–7

2. Maximum pension available to the worker (and dependent spouse) whose average wage has been equal to the average male wage in non-agriculture, as a percentage of the average male wage in non-agriculture.

Grade	Criterion	Grade	Criterion
10	96+	5	56–63
9	88–95	4	48–55
8	80–87	3	40–47
7	72–79	2	32–39
6	64–71	1	24–31

3. Maximum pension available to the highest-paid worker (and dependent spouse) as a percentage of the average male wage in non-agriculture.

Grade	Criterion	Grade	Criterion
10	117+	5	52–64
9	104–116	4	39–51
8	91–113	3	26–38
7	78–90	2	13–25
6	65–77	1	0–12

4. Indexing (cost-of-living adjustment).*

Grade	Criterion
10	Automatic, frequent adjustment for changes in wages or prices.
9	Biannual automatic adjustment for changes in wages or prices.
8	Annual automatic adjustment for changes in wages or prices.
7	Annual but not automatic adjustment.
6	Less than annual adjustment.
1	No provision.

5. Degree of means testing.*

Grade	Criterion
10	Universal pension for all citizens, plus supplementary pension for those without pension credits from a public employment-based pension system.
9	Universal pension for all citizens, plus means-tested supplementary pensions for those without additional sources of income.
8	Universal pensions for all citizens but no supplementary pensions for those without additional income.
5	Means-tested minimum pension for all citizens.
1	No minimum.

6. Coverage (old-age pension coverage as percent of population over 15 years of age).*

Grade	Criterion	Grade	Criterion
10	100%	5	50–59%
9	90–99%	4	40–49%
8	80–89%	3	30–39%
7	70–79%	2	20–29%
6	60–69%	1	10–19%

Note: Estimates are from Esping-Andersen (1981). The scale values, determined using criteria somewhat different from Day's, are virtually identical to Day's estimates (except values for Austria and the United States, which are raised somewhat by this procedure).

7. Degree of flexibility in the age at which one qualifies for retirement.*

Grade	Criterion
10	Retirement at age 65 for men and at age 60 for women, or after 35 years of contributions (retirement possible as early as age 50).
8	Early retirement benefits available at four or five years below retirement age.
7	Early retirement benefits available at three years below retirement age.
5	Early retirement or low retirement age for women and for men if necessitated by poor health or unemployment.
4	Early or low retirement age for women only.
3	Retirement at age 65 for both men and women; no early retirement provision.
2	Retirement at an age greater than 65; no early retirement provision.

8. Retirement test—degree of retirement required to qualify.*

Grade	Criterion
10	Retirement not necessary.
8	No retirement test for some categories of workers; reduced benefits for others.
6	Retirement not necessary, but small reduction in benefits in relation to continued earnings.
3	Retirement not necessary, but large reduction in benefits in relation to continued earnings.
2	Substantial degree of retirement necessary.

Chapter
4

The Political Economy of the Citizen's Wage

The aims of this chapter are to outline main theoretical accounts of the development of the modern welfare state and to assess the utility of these accounts in explaining national differences in the quality of public pensions in the capitalist democracies in the postwar period. The general thesis to be advanced is that these differences may be best understood as a product of the underlying conflict to which Marshall (1964: 63) attributed the evolution of social policy more generally in the twentieth century—the ongoing conflict between citizenship and class. The struggle over the entitlements of citizenship, I shall argue, is primarily a struggle between classes. Differences in the quality of citizenship entitlements are the result of the manner in which this struggle has evolved and, especially, the relative balance of power achieved by the two fundamental classes of all capitalist societies—labor and capital. While the thrust of this argument is broadly consistent with the analysis developed in the preceding chapters, it will be useful to briefly summarize several key assumptions on which it rests before we proceed.

Public pension policy, like all welfare-state policy, is part of a larger distributional process that determines the final allocation of a society's wealth and resources. In capitalist societies, the distributional process for most individuals begins in the market—especially the labor market. As Dobb (1946) argues, capitalism begins with the establishment of a labor market, a form of economic organization that transforms labor into a commodity to be bought and sold for a wage. It is from this wage relationship that the fundamental cleavage of a capitalist economy emerges—between those who sell labor and those who purchase it. Like the sellers of any commodity, those who sell labor power seek to maximize its price; those who purchase labor seek to minimize its price. The wage relationship also determines the structure of power and control under capitalism. As Stephens (1979: 32) observes, since labor "in advanced capitalism is in a seller not a buyer role . . . it takes orders rather than issues them when it is employed."

But in the area of distribution (wages), rarely has labor been the passive object of capitalist rule. Through collective organization in unions, workers are able to enhance their bargaining power vis-à-vis employers and to demand wage levels beyond those which would normally prevail in the unfettered free market envisioned by Adam Smith. As Stephens (1979: 10) notes:

> When the workers stage the first successful strike, the social order in question can no longer be said to be a "purely capitalist" social order . . . [since] there no longer exists a pool of free labourers in competition with one another for a few scarce jobs. The workers, at least some of them, have put an end to competition among themselves . . . .

It is not only in the labor market that workers can use their potential organizational power to alter the structure of distribution. Once the liberal state became the liberal democratic state, it was possible for workers, in their capacity as citizens, to alter the dispersal of resources through political influence and direct control of the state (by means of their own political parties). Because of the separation of state and economy in capitalist democracies, workers are able to alter the distributional process in a manner that is independent of market criteria and the class principle; in effect, the market can be bypassed, and its rules of distribution made irrelevant.[1]

It is from within this larger context that we must view the evolution of old-age pension entitlements in the postwar capitalist democracies. Since the 1940s, the issue of old-age pensions has become firmly embedded in the larger struggle for the wages of labor. Private pensions simply became part of the larger wage package to be negotiated at the bargaining table. Wage settlements increasingly took the form of a trade-off between current wages to be consumed today and deferred wages to be consumed after retirement. And, though administered by the state, public pensions were also drawn into the wage-setting process.

In Europe, expanded public pension programs were frequently negotiated as part of a larger national wage package—a "social contract" between employers' associations, central labor organizations, and the state to exchange wage demands for improved social benefits, including old-age entitlements (Gough, 1979: 148). In

Canada, as Murphy (1982) documents, the Old Age Security Act of 1951 was in large measure a response to demands from Canadian industrialists faced with the prospect of providing the full cost of the retirement wage as a result of demands from organized labor at the bargaining table. In 1950, the *Financial Post*, Canada's leading business newspaper, pointed out the obvious advantage of a universal program to employers: "The more Ottawa pays, the less will be demanded of them" (quoted by Murphy, 1982: 21).

As employers in Canada and the United States soon recognized, however, expanded public pensions did not reduce the wage bill for the economy as a whole but simply spread the costs. An increase in the retirement wage, whether public or private, was in the final analysis a wage increase that had to be financed out of current or future production. Any increase in public or private retirement benefits that was not met by a corresponding reduction in current real wages represented a wage gain for labor and a wage cost for employers.

In effect, the growth of public entitlements meant that the size and distribution of the national wage bill was becoming increasingly determined by the interaction of political and market forces, rather than by market forces alone. Public pension benefits—a deferred wage—became part of a broader wage-setting process mediated by the state. As such, these benefits became subject to the same influences that affect the overall wage-setting process. In the market, wage levels reflect bargaining power: powerful labor unions are usually able to demand and get higher wages and more generous pension entitlements. In a parallel fashion, it is the relative bargaining power of labor inside the state—political power—that is crucial in determining the quality of the citizen's wage. The more influence and control labor is able to exert in the political process, the greater the likelihood it will win a generous set of public pension entitlements.

The origins of this argument are to be found in a larger body of theory and research on the political and economic performance of the postwar capitalist democracies. The common strand of this "new political economy" perspective (Hollingsworth and Hanneman, 1982) is the central role given to the balance of class forces in explaining the differential development of the political and economic institutions of these countries (Hewitt, 1977; Hibbs, 1977; Korpi, 1980; Stephens, 1979). The elements of this argument are developed below in the context of the broader theoretical debates from which it has emerged. In the course of this discussion, a number of alternative and competing explanations of the distributional practices of the contemporary welfare state are also introduced and empirically assessed.

Democracy, Class, and the Politics of Distribution

The idea that the rise of universal suffrage and mass democracy would bring with it a great leveling of social inequalities was firmly rooted in nineteenth-century social thought. The assumption that mass democracy and a capitalist economy were fundamentally incompatible forms of organization was shared by both conservatives and radicals. With general enfranchisement, it was thought, the impoverished majority would seize control of the state and use it as an instrument to counteract the inegalitarian effects of the market. The fact that the advent of democracy did not lead to the immediate demise of capitalism clearly necessitated a revision of these expectations. Democracy had to be reassessed, and we may usefully distinguish among current theories of the welfare state by reference to the various directions in which this reassessment has led.

According to some theorists, the advent of democracy did make a difference in the distributional practices of the capitalist economies. If capitalism was not abolished, it was at least transformed. Among the more influential proponents of this position is Gerhard Lenski (1966). For Lenski, the key to understanding distributive systems is power (1966: 44); the fundamental division in all societies is between those who have and those who do not have power. With power come privilege and access to the good things in life. Lenski's basic model of the distributive process is derived from the classical theory of elites, as found in the writings of Mosca, Pareto, and Weber. But in contrast to these theorists, Lenski argues that the advent of democracy transformed the distribution of power. As a result, the long-term trend toward increasing inequality was reversed. For the first time, the many were able to "combine against the few, and even though individually the many are weaker, in combination they may be as strong or stronger" (Lenski, 1966: 318). Thus, although capitalism is not overthrown, political democracy permits the many to alter the distribution of life chances through their own political efforts. Where political democracy has taken hold, it has tended to result in significant shifts toward equality (the principle of citizenship) via the instrumentality of state policies.

For the adherents of this "simple democratic" hypothesis, as Hewitt (1977) has called it, the causes of variations in the distributive policies of democratic states are considered to be largely endogenous to the political process. There are, however, several views of the manner in which this occurs. Part of Lenski's formulation focuses on the extensiveness of political *rights*—the degree to which access to political office is democratically controlled (popular sovereignty) and political and civil liberties guarantee the right to engage in organized political opposition. Democracy, then, is defined primarily in terms of structures that minimize the power of the elite and maximize that of the non-elite (Bollen, 1980: 372). It is this aspect of Lenski's argument that figured most prominently in the early analyses of public policy and redistribution (Cutwright, 1967a, 1967b). In this formulation, *the quality of citizenship entitlements is a function of the degree to which the power of the elite is circumscribed by formal democratic institutions* (Hypothesis 1).

For other democratic theorists, however, democracy is defined not in terms of structure but in terms of process. Democracies are about elections: the more competitive the electoral process, the more responsive political elites must be to the demands of the electorate in order to reach and remain in office. The tradition of defining democracy in terms of electoral competition has an illustrious lineage. Dating from Schumpeter (1950) and an elaboration by Downs (1957), this perspective has found new expression in recent theories of the "political business cycle" (Tufte, 1978). In this view, rather than being in conflict with the market, democracy is the political analog of the market. Political parties, like firms, compete with one another in the pursuit of customers (voters). When competition is intense, parties must attempt to maximize their appeal, especially to the "have-not" voters (Key, 1949), by promising greater spending on programs of direct benefit to them. *Thus, the more intensive the electoral competition, the higher will be the quality of citizenship entitlements* (Hypothesis 2). Social programs that benefit the elderly are a case in point. Throughout the postwar period, promises to improve pension benefits became a favorite electoral platform among political parties of all stripes. As Tufte (1978: 30) documents, nine out of thirteen legislated postwar increases in U.S. Social Security benefits occurred in election years, and election-year increases were typically higher than those of non-election years.

In the more extreme expressions of the simple democratic thesis, the problem of class seems to disappear altogether. Or if it is retained, classes are reduced to one set of interest groups among others that compete for the attention of the democratic state. It is as though the rights and privileges that stem from the class principle (property ownership) are removed from the political process once mass democracy is achieved. There is certainly no sign of the systematic conflict between class and citizenship discussed by Marshall. Or, where Marshall's analysis is considered (Bendix, 1964; Parsons, 1971), it is given a rather one-sided reading. As Goldthorpe observes (1978: 202), these authors have emphasized Marshall's discussion of citizenship rights as a potential mechanism of social integration and "class abatement" while ignoring his observations concerning the continuing conflict between social rights and market value. In effect, simple democratic theory may be read as a "radical" democratic theory, one in which the class axis of the political process is all but abolished by mass democracy.

Lenski, however, suggests that a simple democratic account overlooks several basic features of the electoral process. The democratic state is an instrument of power and, in Lenski's language, an object of struggle (1966: 318). But the institution of private property biases this struggle in favor of the propertied class (Lenski, 1966: 318) simply because electoral constituencies are large and so elections are costly. Accordingly, those elected to high public office must be wealthy in their own right or be financed by persons of wealth. For persons of modest means, the only compensating power resource is mass organization in a socialist or a labor party. Only if the working class organizes as a class and uses its electoral strength to elect socialist governments will the potential of democracy to expand citizenship entitlements be realized.

These themes, which remain somewhat peripheral to Lenski's analysis, become the foundation of the new political economy. Like Lenski, Korpi (1980) begins with the assumption that the distributive process is rooted in the distribution of power. The distribution of power resources is, in turn, related to class structure. In a capitalist society, the class structure results in two broad types of power resources: "on the one hand, power resources based on the control over the means of production and, on the other hand, power resources based in organizations which can coordinate and control the 'human capital' resources of individual wage-earners into collective action, that is primarily unions and political parties" (Korpi, 1980: 298). For Korpi and for others who follow this school of thought (for example, Stephens, 1979), the key to understanding cross-national differences in the social policies of the capitalist democracies is to be found in the degree to which wage-earners have been able to mobilize these power resources and, in particular, the degree to which working-class parties have made effective use of the franchise to achieve electoral victory. Thus, *variation in the quality of citizenship entitlements in the capitalist democracies is a function of the level of the economic and political power achieved by working-class organizations* (Hypothesis 3). As Hewitt (1977: 451) contends: "The crucial matter is what the mass electorate does with the franchise and other democratic procedures. Only if the lower classes use their votes to elect socialist governments will democracy result in more equality." For democracy to be an effective instrument of redistribution, it is necessary that the democratic process become explicitly organized along class lines—that workers organize as a class and become represented in the political process as such. In the neo-Marxist expressions of this argument, the welfare state is considered an *effect* of class struggle and variations in welfare-state development are considered a function of the relative power achieved by the working class as a consequence of this struggle (see Gough, 1975, 1979; Esping-Andersen et al., 1976).

It is not sufficient merely to win elections, however. Political power must be stable if it is to be an effective means of implementing and defending citizenship entitlements over time. Alternation in office provides the opposition with the occasion to dismantle past reforms or, more typically, to allow those reforms to erode by failing to make adjustments for social and economic change (Martin, 1973). Alternation in office means a constant series of new beginnings in the pursuit of citizenship. The key to stability is a large, cohesive labor movement capable of providing resources and serving as a continuing basis of political mobilization. A divided union movement will result in a fragmented party. A powerful labor organization, able to mobilize a majority of workers, is also essential to ensure that, once elected, party officials can carry out their mandate. If organized labor is unable to ensure continued success at the polls, the party will of necessity begin to seek out alternative bases of support.

This perspective, then, retains the traditional Marxist emphasis on the role of class and class struggle in explaining social change. But unlike most Marxist theories since Lenin, it takes political democracy seriously. Although democratic political institutions are not a guarantee that social citizenship will be realized, neither do they provide the "best possible political shell" (Lenin) for the reproduction of capitalism. Instead, democratic institutions that allow workers to participate in the political process are seen as potentially in conflict with the institutions of a market economy. Yet such an approach is less optimistic than simple democratic theories of the state, in which mass democracy results in the annihilation of social class as a fundamental axis of political conflict. Rather, mass enfranchisement sets up a tension between two contradictory principles of social organization—one that invests rights in the ownership of property and one that invests rights in persons as members of a social community.

Political Democracy, Class Power, and the Citizen's Wage: An Empirical Assessment

We are now in a position to present a preliminary account of cross-national differences in the quality of pension entitlements in the capitalist democracies. To what extent do the insights embodied in the hypotheses outlined above enable us to explain the differences in the quality of public pension entitlements described in Chapter 3? To test these hypotheses, we must first develop one or more operational indicators for each of the key concepts that enter into the major propositions of these perspectives. Having done so, we shall then be able to evaluate the empirical adequacy of these alternative accounts.[2]

Political Democracy and Electoral Competition

The empirical analysis of the effects of political democracy on redistribution and social entitlements has had a contentious history. Cutwright (1967a, 1967b) found evidence that the presence of formal democratic institutions was associated with a lower level of inequality and a higher level of social program development. Jackman (1975) and Hewitt (1977) rejected these conclusions, but Stack (1978) found evidence in support of Cutwright. Hicks and Swank (1982) also found significant effects of electoral competition on income transfers in the capitalist democracies.

To assess the effects of democratic political rights (Hypothesis 1), we make use of an index recently constructed by Bollen (1980). Like Lenski, Bollen (1980: 372) defines political democracy as "the extent to which the political power of the elite is minimized and that of the non-elite is maximized." The operationalization of this measure is a composite index that incorporates three indicators of popular sovereignty and three indicators of the extent of political liberties.[3] Accordingly, it may be considered an index of the development of *political citizenship* in Marshall's sense of the term.

To measure electoral competition (Hypothesis 2), we measure the voting distribution for each election against the perfectly competitive situation (where each party receives an equal share of the votes).[4] Such figures were tallied for each election between 1945 and 1974, and the median value of the resulting distribution was computed.

Working-Class Power

The postwar success of socialist parties in a number of Western European nations aroused considerable attention among analysts of the "democratic class struggle" (Lipset, 1960). But until the mid-seventies, the likelihood that such parties could actually succeed in restructuring the distributive process was met with considerable skepticism both from the center (Parkin, 1972) and the traditional Marxist left (Miliband, 1969). Social Democratic ideals, it was argued, would flounder on the shoals of the bureaucratic and technological imperatives of a "modern industrial society" (Kerr et al., 1964) or be compromised by the harsh realities of a system of production that remained capitalist (Miliband, 1969; Offe, 1972). In the Anglo-American world, this skepticism was largely the product of the British experience, where the Labour Party was able to achieve only intermittent power and was based in a fractious and divided labor movement. Subsequent empirical work, using a larger cross-national base and a variety of methodologies, has brought this earlier skepticism into question. A high level of working-class power has been shown to be associated with lower levels of unemployment (Hibbs, 1977) and income inequality (Hewitt, 1977; Cameron, 1980) and with higher levels of welfare spending (Stephens, 1979), redistribution (Bjorn, 1979; Hanneman, 1980), and overall size of the public economy (Cameron, 1978).

Measures of working-class power may be divided into three categories: measures of mobilization, measures of labor solidarity (or organizational unity), and measures of labor control over government. Mobilization (Korpi, 1980: 307) refers to the proportion of the labor force organized into unions (economic mobilization) and to the proportion of the electorate that supports working-class parties (political mobilization). A mobilized work force, however, must also be united if it is to transform potential power into actual power. Collective action is weakened if the labor movement is divided into many small units pursuing separate objectives and competing with one another for shares of the total wage bill. To measure the internal cohesion of the labor movement, Stephens's (1979: 93) index of union centralization is used. The index is an additive scale (based on Heady, 1970) that measures the central labor confederation's power over bargaining and strikes, its financial resources, and the size of its staff (see also Wilensky, 1976). Decentralized systems are those in which bargaining takes place at the firm or establishment level; the most highly centralized are those where bargaining is economy-wide—that is, where a central labor organization negotiates labor contracts for the entire work force with a parallel employers' association.

Labor control over government is measured by the number of years in the postwar period during which the executive function (i.e., the cabinet) was controlled by labor parties. Stephens (1979: 91) measures the level of socialist rule in the capitalist democracies with an additive index that assigns a score of one for each year between 1945 and 1970 in which the executive function was controlled by socialist (Social Democratic or Communist) parties. For coalition governments that include socialist parties, a fraction is assigned based on the proportion of parliamentary seats held. A similar measure has been constructed by Korpi and Shalev (1980) for the period up to 1975. The results with both measures are identical, and only those using Stephens's index are reported here. Similarly, Stephens's indicators of economic mobilization (percent unionized) and political mobilization (average percentage of votes for left parties, 1945–1970) are used for purposes of presentation.

Results

Table 4.1 gives the zero-order correlations of the index of pension quality with the six independent variables described above.[5] The full correlation matrix appears later in this chapter as Table 4.5. Two estimates for each bivariate correlation are presented—one set with Australia included and one set with Australia excluded. Because of Australia's extreme value on the index of pension quality, this country proved to be an outlier in all of the models to be presented below, an exception for which our models cannot account. This could be the result of inadequate theory, inadequate measurement, or both.

With or without Australia, two of the three hypotheses are supported by this analysis; and when Australia is excluded, Hypothesis 1 just fails to meet the conventional .05 level of significance.[6] The

Table 4.1
Democracy, Class, and the Quality of Public Pensions: Zero-Order Correlations

Hypothesis	With Australia		Without Australia	
	r	Hypothesis supported	r	Hypothesis supported
1. Political democracy	.19	no	.37[a]	just fails
2. Electoral competition	.46[b]	yes	.47[b]	yes
3. Working-class power				
Socialist rule	.64[c]	yes	.69[c]	yes
Socialist vote	.29	no	.50[b]	yes
Union membership	.50[b]	yes	.67[c]	yes
Union centralization	.63[a]	yes	.67[c]	yes

[a] $p < .10$
[b] $p < .05$
[c] $p < .01$

largest correlations are between the index of pension quality and the several indicators of working-class power. These results suggest that a well-organized and cohesive labor movement that is able to achieve control over the government for extended periods of time is the best guarantor of high-quality pensions. The collinearity among the various indicators of working-class power and the small sample size make it impossible to confidently identify the separate effects of these variables within a single equation. When any of the other variables were entered into the same equation, however, the strongest of the four indicators was the index of socialist rule. Given the nature of the dependent variable, one would expect this outcome. A strong and cohesive labor movement is more able to mobilize electoral support for working-class parties, but it is the success of such parties in achieving control over the state that is crucial for the policy-making process.

Further inspection of the data indicates that the presence of a highly unified labor movement (union centralization) accounts for some of the anomalies that emerge when the level of socialist rule is considered alone. Consider Table 4.2, where the 15 countries are grouped according to levels on both variables. Of the seven countries in Table 4.2 with moderate to strong socialist rule and moderate to strong union centralization, only Belgium fails to fit the pattern of high scores on the index of pension quality. Finland and the Netherlands, which have high scores on the index of pension quality but where socialists have had moderate to low representation in cabinet, are both characterized by highly centralized labor movements.

The small sample size and the collinearity between these two variables preclude the possibility of making precise estimates of the separate effects of these two forms of working-class power. As a second-best solution, a composite index of working-class power was constructed by weighting the index of socialist rule with the index of union centralization.[7] As indicated by the values of R^2 in Table 4.3, this method led to some improvement in the fit of the model, but more instructive is the comparison of the residuals for each country. A residual is the difference between the value *observed* on the index of pension quality and the value *predicted* by the regression equation. A negative residual indicates that the country in question has a lower score on the index of pension quality than that predicted by the equation, and a positive residual indicates a higher score than that predicted.

A comparison of the first and second columns of Table 4.3 indicates that the weighted index leads to a substantial improvement in fit for the United Kingdom, Denmark, the Netherlands, and Sweden. Very simply, this means that taking into account the highly

Table 4.2
Socialist Rule, Union Centralization, and Pension Quality in 15
Capitalist Democracies

	Socialist rule	Centralization	Pension quality
1. Strong socialist rule and high centralization:			
Sweden	24	30	186
Norway	20	30	158
2. Moderate socialist rule and high centralization:			
Finland	9	25	168
The Netherlands	6	33	147
Austria	10	35	145
Belgium	9	30	124
3. Strong socialist rule and moderate centralization:			
Denmark	16	15	144
4. Moderate socialist rule and low centralization:			
New Zealand	7	0	136
United Kingdom	12	0	111
5. Low socialist rule and low centralization:			
Canada	0	0	134
France	4	3	131
United States	0	0	120
Switzerland	0	5	118
Germany	3	5	115
Australia	5	4	79

centralized labor movements of Sweden, Denmark, and the Netherlands improves our ability to explain the high scores of these countries on the index of pension quality; the absence of a centralized and cohesive labor movement in the United Kingdom improves our ability to account for this nation's very low level of pension quality. In contrast, the relative underdevelopment of Belgian pension policy becomes even more of a problem when the combined effects of socialist rule and union centralization are considered.

Overall, however, Hypothesis 3 does rather well in accounting for the quality of old-age benefits in the capitalist democracies. A cohesive labor movement that is also able to win electoral victory and sustain political control for extended periods of time appears to

Table 4.3
Residuals from the Regression of the Index of Pension Quality on
Socialist Rule and Socialist Rule Weighted by Union Centralization

		Residuals	
		Socialist rule	Weighted index of working-class power
Austria		3.7	−5.9
Belgium		−15.2	−21.0
Canada		12.7	10.1
Denmark		−9.2	1.6
Finland		28.8	26.4
France		1.7	5.8
Germany		−12.2	−10.4
The Netherlands		13.8	6.9
New Zealand		0.8	11.1
Norway		−3.2	−10.4
Sweden		16.8	9.0
Switzerland		−3.2	−6.2
United Kingdom		−34.2	−13.6
United States		−1.2	−3.8
	$\bar{R}^2 =$	.48	.66

provide an effective means of achieving a high level of income protection for retired workers.[8]

The simple democratic theory of the distributive process also receives some support from Table 4.1. The indicator of postwar electoral competition is significantly correlated with pension quality (Hypothesis 2), and the relationship with Bollen's index of political rights (Hypothesis 1) just fails to meet conventional levels of significance when Australia is excluded. The effect of formal democratic political rights (if any) is entirely indirect, however. Bollen's index of political rights is associated with higher levels of working-class mobilization and power (see Table 4.5), and its relationship with pension quality disappears ($b^* = .05$) when it is entered into a multivariate equation that controls for working-class power.[9] Although the evidence is weak, the underlying process would appear to be one in which political rights enhance social rights by facilitating working-class mobilization and control of government, as anticipated by the classical theorists.

In contrast, the effect of electoral competition remains significant ($b^* = .29$) at the .05 level even after controlling for the weighted index of working-class power. Faced with a high level of competition at the polls, it would appear that parties do indeed bid up the quality of pension entitlements in the pursuit of votes.

The structure of these data, then, is consistent with the overall pattern of postwar policy making described above. Where labor has been successfully mobilized into cohesive working-class organizations, and especially where this strength has been translated into political power, the quality of public pensions for the elderly has been enhanced. The intensity of electoral competition also appears to have made a difference. Democracy provides not only the conditions that allow the "many to combine against the few," but also a process that requires the few to heed the demands of the many.

While this discussion provides a plausible account of the differential development of old-age pensions in the postwar period, it hardly exhausts the range of alternative and competing theories. Before discussing the broader implications of these findings, we must determine whether or not this preliminary assessment of the importance of the "democratic class struggle" requires modification in light of other factors that constrain and determine the formation of social policy in the capitalist democracies.

Labor Militancy and Mass Turmoil

The underlying premise of the new political economy is that the quality of citizenship entitlements reflects the capacity of organized labor to impose its demands on the political system. Despite this assumption, research in this tradition has given scant attention to a form of working-class power that in the Anglo-American democracies is most typically associated with a strong labor movement—namely, the power to disrupt the system through strike activity, political protest, and violence. The tendency to overlook the influence of "extra-institutional" forms of power and influence (Hicks and Swank, 1982) stands in stark contrast to a prominent tradition in American literature that attributes all welfare-state reforms to such factors. The classical statement of this view is found in *Regulating the Poor*, by Piven and Cloward (1971). State policies that benefit the masses, they argue, are temporary concessions granted by elites in the face of destabilizing social changes (such as depressions) that threaten the established order and the legitimacy of elite power. The key force that generates the rise and fall of welfare-state expenditures is mass turmoil (strikes, riots, and other collective social disturbances), which signals to the elite that something must be done if order is to be restored and the system maintained. A case in point is the U.S. Social Security Act of

1935, which in this view is explained as a symptomatic response by elites in the United States to the turmoil (including the old people's movement) brought on by the Great Depression. From this perspective, *the key to explaining differences in the quality of citizenship entitlements is to be found in differences in the level and intensity of civil unrest* (Hypothesis 4). Ruling elites in all societies, democratic or otherwise, grant redistributive concessions only when faced with the threat of imminent demise. And when the threat has passed, the concessions are usually withdrawn.

This perspective has received less than serious consideration from the new political economy theorists for several reasons. First, the mass-turmoil thesis assumes that the course of history is determined largely, if not uniquely, by the interests and decisions of the ruling elite or the capitalist class (see Dye and Zeigler, 1975: 6). The capitalist class or the ruling elite are ultimately the winners in all social confrontations; they experience no contradictions or long-term losses. Power moves only from the top down: the working classes or masses are the passive recipients of elite decisions. In this respect, the thesis has more in common with the static, power-elite models of Pareto, Mosca, and Michels than with the dialectical model of class struggle that is used by the new political economy theorists. Second, in the latter perspective strikes and social unrest are generally construed as an indicator of a weak rather than a strong working class. It is argued that workers resort to such "extra-institutional" forms of political influence only when they are denied direct access to the levers of power. Both longitudinal and comparative studies of strike activity indicate that the volume of strike activity is inversely related to working-class control of the state (Hibbs, 1978; Korpi and Shalev, 1980). This pattern is also evident in our data.

To measure the level of *strike activity*, we have used Korpi and Shalev's (1980: 313) index of relative strike involvement (number of strikers relative to the non-agricultural work force) for the period 1945–1976. The magnitude of *civil protest* is measured using data from Gurr (1978) and is equal to the product of participants times duration of protest per 100,000 non-agricultural workers averaged over the period 1960–1970.[10] There are modest negative correlations of both measures with the indicators of working-class power. The correlation of the weighted index of working-class power with the level of strike involvement is −.37, and with the magnitude of civil protest, it is −.21. Not surprisingly then, both measures have a modest negative correlation with the index of pension quality (−.07 and −.09). But it may be premature to conclude that mass turmoil and labor militancy have no impact—or even a negative impact—on the quality of public entitlements. In those countries where the working class does not have a high level of institutionalized control over the political process, strikes and various other disruptive activities may well acquire the significance that Piven and Cloward attach to them. The extent of their significance can only be determined by a multivariate analysis that simultaneously controls for working-class power and social unrest. Swank (1981) and Hicks and Swank (1982) have found that once controls are made for working-class power inside the state, there is a positive and significant effect of economic unrest (strikes) on welfare-state expenditures. The results here parallel these findings. After controlling for working-class power, the standardized regression coefficient from the regression of pension quality on strike activity is .26, which just fails to meet the conventional .05 level of significance. Thus, it would appear prudent not to reject this hypothesis out of hand. The multivariate analysis suggests that, in the absence of more direct forms of power, the capacity to affect political outcomes by disrupting economic activities may be a non-trivial source of working-class influence. Such a conclusion also seems warranted in light of parallel findings by Swank (1981) and by Griffin, Devine, and Wallace (1980), which show that in the United States (where direct labor control of government is weak) strike activity and racial insurgence have had significant effects on social outlays during the postwar period.

The End of Politics:
Functionalist Theories of the Welfare State

"Structural-functionalist" theories, both Marxist and non-Marxist, have occupied an especially prominent place in contemporary analyses of the welfare state. The distinguishing feature of all such theories is the negligible role played by the political process per se in explaining welfare-state policies. Rather, the state is conceived of as passively responding in a predictable fashion to the functional imperatives generated by the underlying structure of the larger society. We shall consider two variants of this perspective: the welfare state as the inevitable outcome of the "logic of industrialism" and as an expression of the "logic of capitalism."

In the customary presentation of sociological theory, the term "structural functionalism" is employed to distinguish a large body of classical and contemporary mainstream sociological theories of society from the Marxist, or "conflict," tradition. But this is not a very useful distinction, as Giddens (1976: 716–722) has pointed out. First, the term structural functionalism refers to a logical form of argument found in both Marxist and non-Marxist theories. Second, what

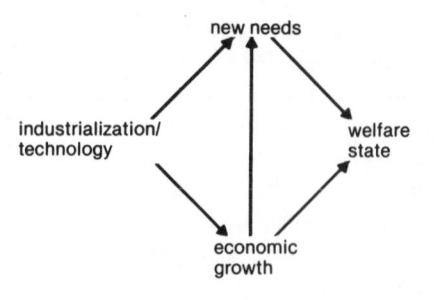

*Figure 4.1   Schematic Representation
of the "Logic of Industrialism" Thesis*

distinguishes these two traditions is more properly found in the substantive content of the theories in question.

Giddens (1976: 718) argues that the substantive core of the so-called structural-functionalist perspective, from Comte to Parsons, is the *theory of industrial society*. The modern era is not to be understood in terms of the emergence of capitalism as in the Marxist paradigm but, rather, in terms of the transition from agricultural to industrial society. It is the "logic of industrialism" that moves and transforms modern societies (Kerr et al., 1964). All social institutions, including welfare institutions, have been transformed in response to the technological imperatives of industrial production by virtue of an increased capacity to respond to these new needs as a result of the new wealth and relative affluence produced by industrialization. A simple schematization of this model is presented in Figure 4.1.

With industrialization comes the need for an educated and mobile labor force. Urbanism, the necessary correlate of industrialism, produces new health problems and creates new housing and transportation requirements. Systems of social support based on kinship and the patrimonial customs of loyalty and deference break down. The result, as Kerr et al. (1964: 22, 152) observe, is a new and expanded role for the state, in which it must maintain the work force and achieve coordination and consensus—a formulation not unlike that of the Marxist theorists to be discussed below. The force of these structurally generated imperatives results in the demise of politics as a key independent force in producing social change. There is an "end of ideology" (Bell, 1960), since the logic of industrialism compels all societies to proceed along a similar evolutionary path. Because of these imperatives, all industrialized nations (communist and capitalist) have produced a virtually identical array of social-welfare provisions for their citizens—workers' compensation, old-age insurance, and sickness and unemployment benefits. The expansion of these

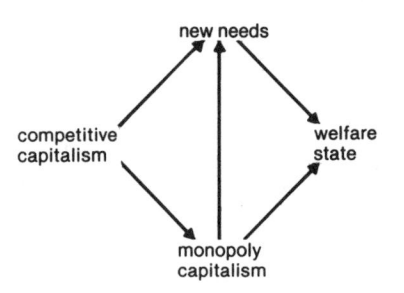

Figure 4.2   Schematic Representation
of the "Logic of Capitalism" Thesis

welfare provisions is facilitated by the new wealth and expanded surplus, which is made available by the increased productivity that accompanies industrialization (Pryor, 1968; Wilensky, 1975). In turn, expanded wealth may create additional needs that require welfare effort. Improvements in nutrition and health care, for example, may increase the size of the elderly population (Wilensky, 1975).

A parallel explanation of the development of the welfare state is to be found in traditional Marxist accounts (see Figure 4.2). According to the Marxist formulation, the capitalist state is driven not by the logic of industrialism but by the *logic of capitalism*. The new needs that result from industrialization are not due to industrial production per se but are shaped and molded—given content—by the relations of production peculiar to industrial capitalism. Old age, for example, becomes a problem because of the commodification of labor, making the mass of the population dependent on the wage relation and the labor market for survival. For those who do not have access to the labor market (such as the aged), survival becomes a problem. But their survival is also a problem for capitalism. A minimum level of social cohesion and stability must be maintained for production to go on, and such stability is unlikely to be a characteristic feature of a society where most people are faced with the threat of impoverishment when they are sick, old, or unemployed. A major task of the capitalist state, therefore, is to manage this inherent contradiction between the *accumulation requirements* of capital, on the one hand, and the *legitimation* of this mode of production, on the other (O'Connor, 1973). The result is the welfare state—a systematic response to the functional imperatives created by the logic of capital accumulation. Commenting on the growth of public expenditures for the elderly, O'Connor (1973: 138) writes:

> the primary purpose of the system is to create a sense of economic security within the ranks of employed workers . . . and thereby raise

morale and reinforce discipline. This contributes to harmonious management—labor relations which are indispensable to capital accumulation
and the growth of production.

The conceptual analog to economic development in Marxist theory is
the transition from competitive to monopoly capitalism—the emergence of "big business," which results from the increasing concentration and centralization of capital characteristic of all capitalist
societies. Indeed, the welfare state is the child of the monopoly
sector. As O'Connor observes (1973: 8), "The growth of the monopoly sector is irrational in the sense that it is accompanied by
unemployment, poverty, economic stagnation, and so on. To insure
mass loyalty and maintain its own legitimacy, the state must meet
various demands of those who suffer the 'costs' of economic growth."
For O'Connor, then, "the growth of state spending is the result of the
growth of the monopoly industries" (1973: 8). In sum, economic
growth is accompanied by a whole series of social dislocations that
require more and more state intervention. Firms in the monopoly
sector are generally successful in influencing the state to absorb more
and more of their real costs of production (including a substantial
portion of the wage bill) through such devices as socialized health care
and social security programs.

The implication of the industrialization thesis is that differential
levels of relative affluence account for differential entitlements for
the aged, the infirm, and the unemployed. The level of state
redistribution is simply a function of the size of the social surplus
available for such purposes. Thus, *the higher the level of economic
development, the higher the quality of citizenship entitlements* (Hypothesis 5).
To assess this hypothesis, we follow the conventional practice of
measuring economic development with Gross Domestic Product
(GDP) per capita.[11] From the Marxist variant of this thesis, we can
deduce that *the quality of citizenship entitlements will be higher in those
capitalist democracies where the process of capital concentration and centralization (monopolization) is most advanced* (Hypothesis 6). Monopolization is
measured with Stephens's (1979) estimates, based on indicators
constructed by Pryor (1973).[12]

Finally, both perspectives converge in assigning independent
effects to the volume of demand for such entitlements. The industrialization theorists typically refer to the level of *need* (the number
of unemployed, elderly, etc.), whereas neo-Marxists emphasize the
expanding *surplus population* (O'Connor, 1973) produced by the growth
of the monopoly sector. Among the motors that drive the development of the welfare state is the systematic tendency of monopoly
capital to substitute capital for labor, thereby destroying jobs and
driving down the relative demand for labor. The result is a growing

Table 4.4
Functionalist Theories of the Citizen's Wage

	Standardized regression coefficients	
Hypothesis	Zero-order	Controlling for working-class power
5. Economic development	−.02	−.02
6. Monopolization	.50[a]	.16
7. Population 65 +	.05	−.45[a]

[a]$p < .05$

surplus population—a postindustrial proletariat dependent on the state, which neither participates in the labor market nor competes for the jobs of those who do (O'Connor, 1970). The elderly represent one, albeit a significant, sector of this dependent population that the state supports in order to underwrite the human costs of monopoly sector growth. Thus, *the larger the dependent population, the higher the quality of citizenship entitlements* (Hypothesis 7). Demand for pension benefits is measured by the percentage of the population over the age of 65 in each country.

Table 4.4 presents the standardized regression coefficients from the regression of the index of pension quality on the three measures discussed above, both before and after controlling for working-class power. None of the hypotheses are supported. At the zero-order level, there is a significant correlation with the level of monopolization, but this relationship disappears after the measure of working-class power is entered into the equation. This result is similar to that reported by Stephens (1979). He observes that the effects of monopolization on welfare-state development are indirect. Following Marx, Stephens argues that increased capital concentration brings workers together in fewer and fewer work units, increasing the level of communication and interdependence between them and thus contributing to the emergence of a stronger and more unified labor movement. This conclusion is clearly indicated by the strong positive relationships between the index of monopolization and the indicators of working-class power (see Table 4.5). But such a process is quite different from that which the "logic of capitalism" school suggests is the basis of the expansion of the welfare state. Rather, Stephens's analysis of the relation between monopolization and welfare-state development is simply a specification of the process that underlies the emergence of working-class power.

Table 4.5
Correlations, Means, and Standard Deviations (S.D.)[a]

	1	2	3	4	5	6
1. Pension quality	—	.64	.29	.50	.63	.75
2. Socialist rule	.69	—	.69	.87	.60	.87
3. Socialist vote	.50	.74	—	.61	.44	.51
4. Percent unionized	.67	.89	.61	—	.66	.83
5. Union centralization	.67	.58	.49	.69	—	.83
6. Working-class power (weighted index)	.81	.86	.56	.86	.83	—
7. Political democracy	.37	.44	.31	.54	.37	.40
8. Electoral competition	.47	.10	.37	.02	.37	.24
9. Strikes	−.07	−.24	.07	−.43	−.33	−.37
10. Civil unrest	−.10	−.17	.10	−.46	−.23	−.21
11. Monopolization	.50	.41	.42	.54	.43	.46
12. GDP per capita	−.02	−.15	−.63	−.13	−.29	.00
13. Percent 65 +	.05	.54	.51	.48	.41	.49
$\bar{X}$	138.4	8.6	38.1	39.9	15.1	212.5
S.D.	21.5	7.4	14.3	15.6	14.5	254.9

[a]Entries above the diagonal include Australia; entries below the diagonal exclude Australia (see p. 85).

When the level of working-class power is controlled, the effect of a large elderly population is the opposite of that predicted by the theory. Rather than encouraging improvement in public pension policy, a larger elderly population appears to discourage the development of high-quality pensions. In the absence of a political system dominated by the elected representatives of the working class, it would seem that the characteristic political response to a large elderly population is to narrow the social security system for the elderly. This finding, however, should be treated with considerable caution. There are strong positive correlations between the size of the elderly population and the various indicators of working-class strength (see Table 4.5). As a result, the statistical analysis indicated the presence of a collinearity problem, and the separate effects of these variables cannot be reliably estimated.

7	8	9	10	11	12	13	$\bar{X}$	S.D.
.19	.46	−.44	−.03	.41	.00	.28	134.40	25.80
.40	.12	−.28	−.15	.41	−.15	.55	8.30	7.30
.32	.34	.16	.09	.41	−.63	.39	38.70	14.00
.55	.01	−.28	−.46	.54	−.13	.41	40.20	15.10
.33	.38	−.36	−.22	.43	−.28	.44	14.40	14.20
.35	.26	−.40	−.19	.45	.01	.52	200.30	250.10
—	.19	−.17	−.51	.77	−.18	−.24	97.60	3.80
.21	—	.09	.39	.32	−.12	.01	.83	.08
−.39	.24	—	.53	−.23	−.23	−.38	422.00	484.40
−.50	.38	.78	—	−.45	−.04	.19	1053.70	3733.90
.79	.32	−.30	−.45	—	−.21	−.14	1.38	.27
−.18	−.12	−.29	−.05	−.21	—	−.11	3904.00	871.00
−.19	−.05	−.16	.18	−.16	−.13	—	11.60	2.30
97.4	.83	338.6	1125.6	1.38	3909	11.9		
3.9	.07	374.8	3864.1	.28	903	2.1		

This result, moreover, provides a striking contrast to those reported by Wilensky (1975, 1976, 1981), who finds that the size of the elderly population has a strong positive impact on social security spending. Wilensky, however, does not include measures of working-class power comparable to those used here, so the strong positive effect of age composition reported by Wilensky is, arguably, a spurious one.[13] There are a variety of other technical reasons for this discrepancy with Wilensky's findings, but the main conclusion to be drawn, particularly in view of the results of related research (see Stephens, 1979), is that the impact of demography on welfare-state development remains dubious or, at best, indeterminate.

What accounts for the apparent failure of these "grand" theories of modern society to explain national differences in the quality of the citizen's wage? Gough (1979) has suggested several reasons. First, both sets of theories suffer from a theoretical limitation of functional explanations in general. As Gough (1979: 50) observes, the fact that some functions are required of the capitalist state (or the industrial state) tells us nothing about how or when these functions are fulfilled or, more importantly, whether they *are* fulfilled. While structures may create demands, they do not determine whether or how those demands will be met. A second issue concerns the empirical problem these theories were intended to solve—namely, to explain the remarkable social transformations that accompanied the transition from preindustrial to industrial methods of production or, alternatively, from precapitalist to capitalist forms of economic organization. Whether or not these same analytical tools are appropriate for explaining differences *within* these historical types has been the subject of some debate.[14] Operationally, as Jackman (1975) points out, the issue is whether one adheres to a strong (linear) specification of the relation between economic development (or monopolization) and welfare-state development or to a weak (curvilinear) form. The latter specification, for which there is much wider empirical support (Weede, 1980), indicates a ceiling effect—that is, after a certain level of development has been reached, additional economic growth (or monopolization) does not result in further increments in citizenship entitlements. If the curvilinear ("weak") specification is correct, we would anticipate both theories to be of only limited use in explaining current differences in the welfare policies of the advanced capitalist democracies.[15] As Gough (1979: 9) concludes, functionalist theories shed considerable light on the growth of social expenditures in general and on the tendency of social policy in all advanced capitalist countries to converge, but they "cannot satisfactorily explain the immense diversity of social policies which any comparative survey will reveal."

Conclusion

The purpose of this chapter has been to provide an overview of major currents in contemporary analyses of the welfare state and, within the limitations of the available data, to evaluate the relative usefulness of these theories in explaining cross-national differences in the quality of public pensions in the postwar capitalist democracies. The main conclusion of the analysis is that the critical factor accounting for differences in public pension entitlements is the mobilization of the working class and the election to office of working-class parties. The quality of the citizen's wage is in large measure a function of both the degree to which citizens become represented as wage-earners (workers) in the political process and the organization of the political process explicitly along class lines. In the absence of strong working-class organizations, it appears that workers must rely on the less effective mechanism of the strike to achieve their demands.

But if social democracy makes a difference, so too does democracy *tout court*. Formal democratic *structures* do not seem to matter, but a highly competitive democratic electoral *process* does. Faced with the threat of political defeat, parties tend to increase their responsiveness to the demands of the electorate—especially the "have-not" electorate.

It is necessary, however, to acknowledge the historical specificity of these generalizations. The conditions that favored the expansion of the welfare state during the decades following World War II appear, from the vantage point of the eighties, to be historically bounded. By the mid-seventies, welfare-state reform had come to a standstill in most capitalist democracies. While announcements of the death of the welfare state have been premature, it is clear that the citizen's wage now stands at a crossroads. It remains for us to identify both the origins of this condition and the paths that lie open for the future.

Notes

1. There is an implicit assumption here that, given the opportunity, wage and salary workers will choose to alter the distributional outcomes generated by the market. There are two ways of evaluating the plausibility of this assumption. The first is to determine *empirically* what governments ruled by labor and social democratic parties do when they achieve power. The empirical results to be presented in this chapter will speak directly to this point. The second is to theoretically identify the objective interests (if any) that wage and salary workers have in bypassing the marketplace and providing themselves with non-market income entitlements that conform to principles of security, adequacy, and need. This task will be pursued in Chapter 5. Here it can be pointed out that, like any seller of a commodity, wage and salary workers have an objective interest in any arrangement that (1) removes the risk associated with any sudden decline in the market value of that commodity and (2) enhances the purchase price of that commodity. That a generous set of citizenship entitlements provides protection against the first condition should already be apparent. That the welfare state serves to enhance both individual and aggregate wage levels is an issue deferred to Chapter 5.

2. The method used for this empirical assessment, although now conventional in comparative studies of the welfare state (see Wilensky, 1975; Stephens, 1979), is not without difficulties. The reader unfamiliar with

this mode of analysis should be forewarned of these limitations. For each of the major theories identified, one or more key indicators are developed in the form of a quantitative measure. Then the relationship of these indicators to the index of pension quality (Chapter 3) is analyzed by means of bivariate and multivariate regression analysis. The short-comings of this strategy arise from the method itself and from its particular application to the question at hand. As a method, multivariate regression analysis allows us to identify systematic patterns within complex data structures. In practice, theoretical arguments lead us to look for certain patterns in our data. The presence of the expected pattern suggests that the argument may be correct but does not prove it to be so. The discovery of an expected pattern does not demonstrate that the process generating the pattern is the one postulated in the theory, since the same pattern could have been produced by any number of underlying processes. Thus, an analysis such as that presented here can only be assessed in conjunction with a large number of similar studies and detailed case analyses that attempt to study the process directly.

A second set of shortcomings arises from the particular application of the method. First, the data points are a cross-section of 15 capitalist democracies at a single point in time. Thus, we are able to identify systematic patterns that discriminate *between* countries but not patterns that measure changes over time *within* countries. An adequate test of these theories would require an analysis that examines both forms of variation (see Hibbs, 1978, for an example).

Finally, the small number of cases under consideration means that we have a limited amount of information with which to evaluate a large number of theories (in statistical terms, we face a "degrees of freedom" problem) and a statistical procedure that is sensitive to exceptional cases (outliers). Such problems, however, are not solved by detailed com-parative case studies; indeed, the same difficulties appear under a different guise but in a more severe form in such analyses (see Heclo, 1974). Regardless of the method, we are constrained by the fact that the number of advanced capitalist democracies are few and that those for which reasonably comparable data are available are fewer still.

3. The indicators of popular sovereignty include a measure of the fairness of elections and indicators of electoral control over the executive and legislative branches. The three indicators of political liberties are freedom of the press, freedom of group opposition, and government sanctions.

4. The computing formula for this measure is $\Sigma_{i=1}^{N}(P_i - 1/N)^2$ where N is the number of parties competing and P is the proportion of each party's vote. The index has a range from 0 to 1 and takes on a value of 1 when each party receives an equal share of the national vote. Electoral data are from Mackie and Rose (1974).

5. A correlation coefficient (r) is a statistic that measures the degree of association between two variables. A value close to zero indicates that there is little or no association; a value close to 1.00 indicates a nearly perfect association. The sign of the correlation (plus or minus) indicates the direction of association. The associated p-values indicate the proba-

bility that an observed association could be produced by chance. See footnote 6 for further discussion of the issue of statistical significance.

6. Whereas the econometric literature takes the use of significance tests for granted when national data of this type are being used, sociologists trained in the tradition of survey research tend to be more dubious, since no random sample has been drawn. At best, it is possible to claim that significance levels represent the significance of the relationship that would be present had the data been drawn from a simple random sample. Thus, while significance tests may have a heuristic value in the present context, they should not be taken too seriously. In particular, where moderately strong but statistically insignificant relationships appear, the former rather than the latter criterion should be used for assessment.

7. The weighted index is computed by adding 1 to both indicators to eliminate zero scores and then taking the product of the two indicators for each country.

8. It is also apparent that those countries with more developed systems of support for their elderly members are characterized by smaller, more homogeneous populations, which, one might suspect, could lead to fewer internal conflicts between linguistic and ethnic groups and to a greater degree of social solidarity. This atmosphere in turn might produce a greater sense of responsibility toward the elderly regardless of the relative power of the national working class. As Stephens (1979: 111) has shown more broadly in relation to the development of the welfare state, ethnic and linguistic homogeneity does indeed contribute to such development, but in an indirect way, by its effects on the internal cohesion of the working class. Stephens's indices of ethnic and linguistic diversity are significantly correlated with the index of pension quality (−.42 and −.48, respectively), but this effect of population heterogeneity on pension quality is indirect. Ethnic and linguistic diversity has a negative effect on the development of a strong labor movement; once the effects of Socialist Party rule are controlled, however, these factors have no additional impact on the index of pension quality.

9. b^* is a symbol used to denote a standardized regression coefficient. One can usefully think of this as the multivariate analog of the correlation coefficient described in footnote 5—that is, it measures the effect of one variable on another after controlling for the effects of one or more additional variables.

10. Computations for this variable were made available by Duane Swank (see Swank, 1981).

11. The source for this indicator is the *United Nations Statistical Yearbook* (1976). Data are for 1972. None of the usual logged or polynomial transformations of this variable yielded substantively different results from those found with the untransformed measure as presented in the text.

12. Pryor's data cover only ten countries. Stephens used an estimation procedure based on the natural log of GDP to derive estimates for the remaining countries.

13. In his most recent analysis, Wilensky (1981) does employ a measure of "left party dominance," but "left" does not mean socialist as it does here.

For example, in the United States the Democratic Party is designated as "left" by Wilensky, and he characterizes the United States as having a high level of "left party dominance." In contrast, the United States has a score of zero on the index of socialist rule. It is instructive to note, moreover, that among the indicators Wilensky does report as having a significant impact on social security effort is his measure of "corporatism," a weighted index that includes a measure of union centralization.

There are several additional reasons for the discrepancy with Wilensky's findings. The first has to do with the manner in which the dependent variable is measured. Traditional expenditure-based measures of welfare-state development, such as those used by Wilensky, contain a component that incorporates the size of the elderly population (OECD, 1976: 19–20) so that there is an artifactual *positive* correlation between Wilensky's measure of "social security effort" and the size of the elderly population. Second, Wilensky's measure of social security effort also includes health care expenditures, which may respond somewhat differently than do pension benefits to population aging. Third, expenditure-based measures do not take into account the way in which benefits are distributed. The index of pension quality, in contrast, is weighted in favor of those systems which are redistributive from high- to low-income earners.

14. In some formulations, this difference in focus is more than theoretical oversight. Variations within types are effectively defined as nonsystematic (that is, random) and reduced to the level of historical accident (Offe, 1972). The available empirical evidence, however, makes this position difficult to sustain.

15. This discussion also draws attention to the fact that it is necessary to distinguish between the capacity of any of these theories to explain variations *between* countries and changes *within* countries over time. The cross-sectional nature of this analysis precludes the possibility of evaluating the adequacy of any of these theoretical perspectives as explanations of the internal development and growth of the citizen's wage in the capitalist democracies. It is entirely consistent to maintain that the welfare state, as we now know it, would not have developed without the tremendous growth in wealth produced by industrial capitalism in the twentieth century and at the same time to reject the hypothesis that differences between countries at a given point in time can be explained by corresponding differences in relative affluence. Cross-sectional analyses are subject to specification error as a result of omission of the time dimension, but so too are longitudinal analyses that omit the comparative dimension (Rubinson, 1977). The ideal data structure, of course, is a pooled time series that simultaneously allows for estimation of both the within-country (that is, over time) effects and the between-country effects of different variables (for example, see Hibbs, 1978).

Chapter

5

Citizenship at the Crossroads: The Future of Old-Age Security

The apparent success with which the welfare state was grafted to a market economy in the postwar years was seen by many as a sign that a truce had been reached in the ongoing war between citizenship and social class. With an appropriate blend of Keynes and Beveridge, the rights of property and the rights of persons would be reconciled to the advantage of both. Welfare expenditures were construed as an investment in "human capital" that would improve the quality of the work force and reduce the waste of human resources produced by inadequate diet, health care, and education. Public pension systems would help regulate unemployment and allow employers to replace older workers with more efficient, less costly younger workers. Most importantly, redistributive policies would provide the means to regulate the boom-and-bust cycle characteristic of the capitalist economies.

Such optimism was not without foundation. Until the appearance of the massive inflation generated during the Vietnam war and the stagflation that followed the energy crisis of the seventies, both capitalism and the welfare state experienced unprecedented levels of real growth. As the economies of the capitalist democracies grew, expenditures on social welfare grew even faster. Sweden's expenditures on income maintenance rose from 10.5 percent of the Gross National Product (GNP) in 1957 to 30.7 percent in 1977. In the United States, comparable expenditures grew from 5 percent of GNP to almost 14 percent (U.S. Senate Committee on Aging, 1981: 6).*

*Between 1960 and 1978, U.S. federal expenditures on the elderly alone rose from 2.52 percent to 5.3 percent of GNP (Clark and Menefee, 1981: 134).

103

Moreover, the citizen's wage gained considerable ground on the market wage as a primary source of workers' incomes. Bowles and Gintis (1980: 32–37) estimate that over the three decades between 1947 and 1977 the rate of growth of real per capita "citizen's wage expenditures" was five times the rate of growth of real take-home pay in the United States, with the result that social welfare expenditures increased from 11 to 27 percent of total consumption.

In the mid-seventies, however, a contrary view began to take form. The capitalist democracies, it was argued, were suffering from a severe case of democratic overload (Huntington, 1975). The proliferation and growth of citizenship entitlements had created a "revolution of rising expectations" that was now a fetter on capital accumulation. Following the onset of the 1974–1975 recession, there was a growing tendency to regard welfare and efficiency as contradictory, rather than complementary, principles of economic decision making (Geiger and Geiger, 1978: 108). As Heclo (1981: 392) concludes, "What came to be labelled as the welfare state was an arrangement for living with mutually inconsistent priorities, a system of tolerated contradictions."

Within this context, old-age pension systems were candidates for special scrutiny. During the decades following World War II, the rapid growth in old-age security entitlements in all capitalist democracies was widely hailed as a necessary, indeed inevitable, consequence of industrialization and economic growth. Industrialization, it was thought, had simultaneously rendered the labor of older workers redundant and provided the wealth to make their labor unnecessary. A retirement wage sufficient to permit or induce withdrawal from the labor force in advance of physiological decline could, and should, be made available to all. According to the revised view of the seventies, however, a combination of rising entitlements and an increase in the number of retirees was creating a long-term process bound to self-destruct. In the long run, the old-age security systems that were the pride of the postwar welfare state were doomed to collapse under the weight of changing demographic and fiscal realities. The "crisis" of old-age security had been discovered (see Myles, 1981).

The roots of this crisis are usually attributed to demography: the system of old-age security entitlements currently in place in the capitalist democracies simply cannot withstand the projected rise in the number of old people. Wilensky (1975) argued that changing demographic realities gave rise to the modern welfare state; it is now claimed that demography will bring about its demise.

But what is the nature of this demographic imperative? In the pages that follow, I shall propose that the usual formulation of the demographic argument is, at best, highly misleading. This is not to say that demography is irrelevant to our understanding of the current situation. The size and composition of populations represent real constraints on any national political effort, whether for warfare or for welfare. What is required, however, is identification of the forms of social organization and institutional arrangements that make a particular demographic formation into a "problem." I suggest that to understand the current situation we must situate it within the broader context of the postwar welfare state and the political and economic foundations upon which it was constructed. The current conflict over the future of old-age security is a symptom of a larger conflict over the proper role of the democratic state in a market economy. The postwar Keynesian consensus upon which the welfare state was constructed has broken down, with the result that the various social institutions it spawned (including retirement wages for the elderly) have now become the focus of renewed debate and political confrontation. The implication is that the long-term future of old-age security—and hence of old age as we now know it—depends less on innovative fiscal management practices than on the eventual political realignments of a post-Keynesian political economy.

Population Aging and the Crisis in Old-Age Security

The conventional explanation of the crisis of old-age security is a rather straightforward exercise in demographic accounting: the current generation of adults is simply not producing enough children to support it in its old age (Keyfitz, 1980). Because of declining fertility, the size of the elderly population will grow to a point where the economic burden on the young will become intolerable. Eventually the demographic bubble will burst, old-age security programs will go broke, and an intergenerational "class struggle" will ensue (Davis and van den Oever, 1981). To avoid this eventuality, it is argued, people must begin to show restraint now (Clark and Barker, 1981). Promises that future generations will be unwilling or unable to keep should not be made to the current generation of workers (Laffer and Ranson, 1977). In this scenario, we have a social responsibility to dismantle the welfare state for the sake of our children and grandchildren, who must support us in the future.

Several core assumptions underlie this argument. In this view, old-age pensions are not the product of a wage-setting process mediated by the state but the product of an implicit social contract made between sequential age cohorts (Friedman, 1978).[1] Each cohort agrees to support the preceding cohort, under the assumption that it will receive similar treatment from the cohort that follows. But since age cohorts vary in size, the contract is inherently unstable. Although it is relatively easy to provide generous benefits to a small retired population, providing the same benefits to a very large cohort of retirees may become an intolerable burden (Keyfitz, 1980). The result is a conflict between cohorts, leading to dissolution of the contract. It is argued that North Americans can expect such a dissolution when the baby-boom generation retires.

The notion of a social contract between age cohorts is a metaphor intended to enable us to understand and to predict changes in popular support for old-age entitlement programs. The question to be answered is whether the empirical evidence gives any indication that the metaphor is appropriate. Where the conditions specified by the model have been met, it would seem reasonable to expect some evidence of the intergenerational conflict and the resistance to public spending on the elderly that it predicts.

Several Western nations are already quite "old" by demographic standards. The elderly constitute more than 16 percent of the populations of West Germany, Austria, and Sweden—a figure that is not far from the 18 percent at which the North American population is expected to peak in the next century. As Heinz and Chiles (1981: iii) observe:

> Western European social security systems have already experienced the impact of population aging for some time now. The Federal Republic of Germany, for example, currently has a ratio of social security contributors to beneficiaries of less than 2 : 1, which is the level not projected to be reached in the United States until the year 2030, when the postwar baby boom generation reaches old age.

Moreover, the tax burden necessary to finance old-age security in these countries has already reached levels that exceed those projected for North America in the next century. Prior to the amendments of 1983 that reduced the projected costs of the program, the tax rate for U.S. Social Security was projected to peak at 20.1 percent in the year 2035 (Leimer, 1979). But by 1978, the effective tax rate to support old-age security was already 18 percent in Germany, 20 percent in Sweden, 23 percent in Italy, and 25 percent in the Netherlands (Torrey and Thompson, 1980: 43). The experience of these nations, however, provides little evidence of the growing backlash and intergenerational hostility anticipated by the proponents of the conventional view.

Although several countries experienced a "welfare backlash" in the late seventies, Wilensky (1976, 1981) has shown that this pattern was unrelated either to the size of the elderly population or to levels of public spending and taxation. Indeed, according to Wilensky's estimates, the very "oldest" of the capitalist democracies (Germany,

Austria, Sweden) were among the countries that experienced the least amount of popular resistance to rising welfare expenditures. And informed observers (Ross, 1979; Tomasson, 1982) generally agree that, despite *official* concern over rising costs, *public support* of old-age security systems remains high in these countries.

Moreover, where there has been popular reaction against the growth of public spending, support for the elderly appears to occupy a special place. In 1981, only 11 percent of Americans under the age of 65 agreed that Social Security benefits should be reduced in the future. And the majority of those under the age of 65 were prepared to accept further tax increases to keep Social Security viable (Employee Benefit Research Institute, 1981). Coughlin's (1979) comparative review of public opinion poll data indicates that support for old-age security programs is uniformly high and shows little variation from country to country, despite wide differences in the size of elderly populations and in the quality of pension entitlements.

There are some obvious reasons for such widespread support of old-age security, even in the face of rising costs. First, familial bonds provide a strong basis for solidarity between generations. In the absence of suitable public provision for the elderly, adults of working age would be required to provide for their aging parents directly. For these individuals a generous old-age security system is not a burden but relief from a burden. Second, those of working age are generally capable of recognizing that they will require similar support in the future. In the long run, they will suffer if the terms of the "contract" are not met.

Less obvious but perhaps more important is the fact that the key claim of the demographic model—that population aging increases the burden of dependency on the working population—is incorrect. As Table 5.1 demonstrates, population aging has generally been associated with a decline in both total and age-based dependency because of a decline in the size of the very young population and an increase in female labor-force participation. Canadian and U.S. projections indicate a similar trend for the future. Although the size of the elderly population will continue to grow, total age-dependency ratios will first decline and then slowly rise again to current levels (see Table 5.2). At no point are they projected to reach the levels achieved during the early sixties, the peak of the baby-boom period.

The issue for the future, then, is not the *size* of the dependent population but rather its changing *composition*—fewer children and more retirees. The usual strategy in evaluating this change is to compare public expenditures on the old with public expenditures on the young. Since public expenditures on the old amount to approximately three times public expenditures on the young, it is clear that total *public* expenditures on the non-working population must

Table 5.1
Age Dependency and Total Economic Dependency, 1959–1979

	Youth dependency[a] (ages 0–14)		Old-age dependency[a] (age 65+)		Total age dependency[a]		Total economic dependency[b]	
	1959	1979	1959	1979	1959	1979	1959	1979
Australia	30.1	25.7	8.5	9.4	38.6	35.1	n.a.	55.0
Austria	21.8	21.1	12.1	15.5	33.9	36.6	51.8	58.5
Belgium	23.3	20.5	11.9	14.3	35.2	34.8	60.2	58.0
Canada	30.3	23.5	7.8	9.3	38.1	32.8	63.6	52.3
Denmark	25.7	21.3	10.4	14.2	36.1	35.5	54.3	47.9
Finland	30.7	20.6	7.1	11.8	37.8	32.4	52.1	51.6
France	26.1	22.6	11.6	14.0	37.7	36.6	56.3	56.9
Germany	21.0	18.9	10.7	15.5	31.7	34.4	52.0	56.9
The Netherlands	30.0	22.9	8.9	11.4	38.9	34.3	63.2	64.8
Norway	26.1	22.6	10.7	14.6	36.8	37.2	59.2	53.1
Sweden	22.8	20.0	11.6	16.1	34.4	36.1	51.4	48.5
Switzerland	24.0	20.1	10.1	13.7	34.1	33.8	54.0	54.9
United Kingdom	23.2	21.5	11.6	14.7	34.8	36.2	52.5	54.9
United States	30.8	22.8	9.1	11.2	39.9	34.0	60.1	52.4

[a]Defined as a percentage of the total population.
[b]Total non-working population as a percentage of the total population.
Source: Organization for Economic Cooperation and Development *Labour Force Statistics, 1959–70* (Paris: OECD, 1972); *Labour Force Statistics, 1968–79* (Paris: OECD, 1981).

Table 5.2
Projected Age-Dependency Ratios for Canada and the United States

		Dependency ratios[a]		
		Ages 0–17	Age 65 +	Total
Canada	1976	53.5	14.6	68.1
	1986	41.9	16.1	58.0
	2001	36.7	18.5	55.2
	2031	33.3	33.7	67.0
United States	1976	51.3	18.0	69.3
	1985	43.5	19.0	62.5
	2000	43.2	19.9	63.1
	2025	42.0	29.5	71.5

[a]Dependency is defined as a proportion of the working-age population (population aged 18–64).
Sources: Canada: Health and Welfare Canada, *Retirement Age* (Ottawa: Ministry of National Health and Welfare, 1978), p. 17. Reproduced by permission of the Ministre of Supply and Services Canada. U.S.: U.S. Bureau of Census, *Current Population Reports,* "Projections of the Population of the United States: 1977–2050" (Washington, D.C.: U.S. Government Printing Office), Series P-25, No. 704.

increase as the population ages. But to assess the true economic impact on the working population, we must evaluate *total* expenditures on the young and on the old, not just that portion passing through the public purse. Information on this subject is at best incomplete. Based on the analyses of French demographer Alfred Sauvy, Clark and Spengler (1980: 38) conclude that total expenditures on the old exceed those on the young. In contrast, if we accept Wander's (1978) finding that the total cost of raising a child to the age of 20 is one-fourth to one-third *higher* than the total cost of supporting an elderly person from age 60 to death, we can expect that total intergenerational transfers (public plus private) will decline as the population ages.

The empirical foundations for the conventional view, then, appear to be rather shaky. Whatever its consequences, population aging does not seem to be a source of rising economic dependency, intergenerational conflict, or popular backlash against welfare-state spending.[2] This does not mean that the so-called crisis of old-age security is all sound and fury—only that we must look elsewhere to understand its nature and origins.

At the most general level, the current controversy over the future of old-age security is rooted in the broader economic crisis that has beset the capitalist democracies since the early 1970s. A protracted economic slump (characterized by declining output, rising unemployment, and inflation) brought about a radical reassessment of the

postwar welfare state. Rather than a means of reinvigorating capitalism, the welfare state (including the welfare state for the elderly) is
now broadly seen by both the left and the right as a fetter on capital
accumulation (Gough, 1979; Geiger and Geiger, 1978). The crisis in
old-age security is a symptom of this larger crisis of the welfare
state.

The Anatomy of the Crisis

As Geiger and Geiger (1978: 16) observe, the critical issue raised
by the growth of the welfare state is whether or not the market retains
enough of its own output to satisfy its requirements. From the
viewpoint of the marketplace, the portion of the national product
that is administered by the state is "out of control"; that amount is no
longer directly available to provide incentives to labor (in the form of
wages) or to capital (in the form of profits), nor is it directly available
in the form of savings to be used for reinvestment. Access to these
resources is mediated by the state. As a result, their distribution is
subject to the logic of the political process rather than the logic of the
market. The expansion of the public economy increasingly politicizes
economic affairs and, by so doing, reverses the great achievement of
the bourgeois revolutions of the seventeenth and eighteenth cen-
turies—the removal of the state from the realm of economic decision
making (Piven and Cloward, 1982: 42).

Under current arrangements for the distribution of income,
population aging exacerbates this process. Because increased public
expenditures on the elderly are not offset by a corresponding
reduction in public expenditures on the young, population aging
increases the size of the public economy and reduces the share of
national income directly subject to market forces. Thus, although
population aging is unlikely to "break the national bank," it *will* alter
the bank's structure of ownership and control. McDonald and Carty
(1979), for example, estimate that public intergenerational transfers
to the old and young in Canada will rise from 12.8 percent of GNP in
1976 to 17.8 percent of GNP in the year 2031.

But for whom does the expansion of public control over the
distribution of income pose a problem? Any major social transformation is likely to generate conflict between those who stand to
lose and those who stand to gain from such change. The trick is to
identify the probable winners and losers. It is instructive to ask, then,
who stands to benefit and who stands to lose as the result of yet
further expansion of the public economy in general and of the old-age
security budget in particular. If this question can be answered

correctly, we will be in a good position to predict the direction of any conflict that might ensue. More importantly, we will be better able to appreciate the logic of the current controversies and struggles over the future of old-age security.

In the past there have been three quite different answers to the question of who benefits from public control over income distribution. Neo-Marxists have argued that the benefits of the welfare state have gone primarily to the owners and managers of capital; "conservatives" (that is, the proponents of classical liberalism) have argued that the welfare state undermines the power of capital; and the postwar liberals have generally claimed that the welfare state benefits both labor and capital. As Piven and Cloward (1982: 31) point out, however, there is a growing recognition among analysts of all political persuasions that the conservatives were right—the major consequence of the expansion of the public economy has been to alter the structure of power between capital and labor in favor of the latter. Evidence of this shift is found in the market for labor and in the market for capital.

In the labor market, the citizen's wage enhances the bargaining power of labor both individually and collectively. The effects at the individual level have been recognized for some time in the life-cycle model of earnings and labor supply formulated by the Chicago school (for example, see Clark and Barker, 1981). According to this model, individual workers make employment and wage decisions (whether to work and at what wage) according to the anticipated impact of such decisions on total lifetime earnings. Universal income entitlements, such as those typically contained in old-age security provisions, mean that some portion of each individual's total lifetime earnings is fixed by law. Thus, current decisions to work and at what wage can be made in light of the fact that some amount of future income is assured. This assurance reduces dependency on the labor market and enhances the worker's bargaining position with respect to would-be employers. When good jobs at good wages are not available, individuals may simply choose to withdraw, partially or completely, from the labor force. The "work disincentives" that result from the availability of unemployment, sickness, and old-age entitlements reduce the labor supply and drive up wage levels.

To understand the effects of the citizen's wage at the collective level, we must consider the relationship between unemployment and the bargaining power of labor (Piven and Cloward, 1982: 19). Under normal conditions, a rise in unemployment leads to a reduction in wages by increasing the supply of unemployed workers and the subsequent competition for available jobs. But as Bowles and Gintis (1980: 39–48) observe, the citizen's wage increasingly insulates the working class from the reserve army of the unemployed. By absorbing the unemployed, the welfare state also absorbs much of the downward pressure on market wages that an increase in unemployment would otherwise create. Thus, wage levels tend to be higher and profit levels lower than they would otherwise be (see Block, 1981: 15–17). Old-age security provisions are very much part of this process. Among the first to be absorbed in periods of rising unemployment are older workers, who join the ranks of the elderly by moving into early retirement (Clark and Barber, 1981).

From the point of view of employers, this problem is compounded by the fact that the social-wage bill and the market-wage bill are interactive. Unemployment lowers the market-wage bill but simultaneously triggers an increase in the social-wage bill for unemployment, welfare, and retirement benefits. Regardless of how they are financed, public benefits must ultimately be paid for by current production (Wilson, 1974: x). Thus, both market wages and social wages must be construed as a cost of doing business. The problem for employers, then, is that the wage bill as a whole (market wages plus social wages) becomes increasingly rigid and insensitive to market forces.

The problems of employers go beyond the obstacles in the labor market. The effects of the public economy also loom large in the capital market. When the owners and managers of capital attempt to borrow funds to invest in new facilities and equipment or to meet temporary cash-flow problems, they find themselves faced with a very powerful competitor for the supply of available savings—namely, the state. Moreover, state borrowing to finance the public economy tends to increase when individual firms can least afford the resulting rise in interest rates. Downturns in the economy produce rising unemployment, a declining tax base, and an increased level of social spending, thereby increasing government deficits and the need for state borrowing. Increased state borrowing in turn produces the rising interest rates that many firms in recent years have found prohibitive. In the competition for the available pool of capital, governments hold a decided advantage: the state can afford to pay the higher interest rates because of its powers of taxation, which are unavailable to private firms.

The public economy also affects the amount of capital available for investment purposes. Most national pension schemes are funded on a pay-as-you-go basis—that is, current expenditures (benefits) are paid for out of current revenues (contributions). Such a system is a form of pseudo-savings: wage-earners make contributions, but no pool of capital is created. Since these contributions generate income entitlements that can be claimed on retirement, the need for other forms of saving (such as a private pension plan) is reduced. According to Munnell (1981), a dollar of Social Security contributions displaces approximately $0.74 of private pension savings in the United States. But a shift in pension financing from a pay-as-you-go to a funded basis (as practiced in Sweden and Canada) simply compounds the problems of the business community.

As has long been recognized, financing a public pension system on a funded basis results in a significant shift of economic power from the private sector to the state because the capital pool created from contributions is in the hands of government. In Sweden, the National Pension Insurance fund accounts for almost half of total advances on the Swedish credit market (Martin, 1973: 18), effectively nationalizing the flow, if not the stock, of capital. In Canada, the funds of the Canada Pension Plan have become the major source of provincial debt financing. The funds of the parallel Quebec Pension Plan have also been used to finance a state-directed program of private-sector investment. In the latter part of the seventies, recognition of this situation among the Canadian business class resulted in what came to be called the "great pension debate."

Faced with the obvious inadequacies of Canada's old-age security system, Canadian labor proposed, in 1975, to rectify the situation by significantly expanding the Canada Pension Plan. Objections to this proposal had little to do with the need for improvement; and the superiority of the public system over its private-sector counterparts was never seriously questioned. Rather, the principal objection was that such a change would bring about an increase in government control over capital formation. The editors of the Toronto *Globe and Mail* (October 12, 1977) argued: "Government is already too deep into pension plans—and the savings they represent—for the good of Canada's economic future. We need more savings . . . but the savings should be in a variety of hands and not subject to the political vagaries of government." As Murphy (1982) has shown, the reasons for this concern are not difficult to identify. During the decade following the Canada Pension Plan legislation of 1965, corporate savings as a means of amassing new investment capital was in decline and corporations had to turn increasingly to external sources of financing. During the same period, private pension funds grew to become the single largest source of private equity capital in Canada and the major source of corporate borrowing. Expanding the public system further would transfer a significant portion of these savings to the state and, in the words of the *Globe and Mail*, would subject them to the "political vagaries of government." In this way, democratization of the savings and investment process serves to further undermine the power of private capital. Canadian business has made abundantly clear (Business Committee on Pension Policy, 1982) its view that the defense of this power must take precedence over the income requirements of the elderly.

The real crisis in old-age security, then, is an outcome of the adverse effects of the citizen's wage on the power of capital. State intervention to meet social needs created by or not satisfied by the market tends to transform the market itself. When workers in their capacity as citizens can claim a social wage that is independent of the sale of their labor power, capitalist social relations are changed. The "mixed economy" that emerges from this transformation is not a happy marriage between complementary principles of social organization but a unity of opposites, a system of tolerated contradictions. Democratic control over wage and capital formation is the antithesis of capitalist control over wage and capital formation; when the one expands, the other must contract. The principal beneficiary of this shift is labor; the principal losers are the owners and managers of capital. The result is not an intergenerational class struggle but simply an expression of the traditional struggle between labor and capital. The problem is not one of state control per se but, rather, one of *democratic* control of the state. State policies that assign resources on the basis of need and social equality undermine a system of assignment based on property entitlements and market value. The future of old-age security, then, is a problem of democracy, not of demography.

Three Directions for the Future

Following Marshall, I have argued that the present system of old-age security in the capitalist democracies is a product of the attempt to satisfy simultaneously two contradictory principles of social organization. As Marshall anticipated, the social institutions spawned by this union of liberalism and democracy are now on a collision course which has at least three possible outcomes. First, an acute navigator may intervene and avert the collision. If this comes to pass, people will grow old in the future much as they have in the recent past. There will be minor technical adjustments to retirement provisions and old-age security benefits, but nothing substantial will be altered. Second, it is possible that the class principle and the rights of property will be restored to the position of preeminence they held in the past. Such a development would not require abandonment of the retirement principle or the annihilation of social security. Rather, standards of security, adequacy, and need would be abandoned to make the "wages" of the elderly subject to the criteria of distribution that prevail in the market. The third possibility is that the rights of property will be further subordinated to democratic control and the boundaries of the market pushed back so as to reduce and eventually eliminate the source of conflict.[3]

Can the collision be averted? In the current political economy, this is equivalent to asking whether the engines of economic growth can be fired again without a major change in the existing economic order. A survey of recent economic analyses does not offer much hope in this respect (Drucker, 1980).[4] Keynesian theory is in retreat, and the alternatives being advanced generally call for substantial change in the relationship between state and economy upon which the postwar welfare state was constructed.[5]

The second possibility is that neoconservative efforts to roll back history and dismantle the gains in social citizenship achieved during the past several decades will be successful. According to this view, the economic problems of the capitalist democracies are attributable to an "excess of democracy" (Huntington, 1975: 113). The democratic quest for equality has generated "excessive expectations" (Brittan, 1975: 129), a "revolution of rising entitlements" (Bell, 1976: 232) that can no longer be realistically met. As a result, democracy itself is threatened. Usher (1981: 10) states that political democracy is

> unworkable and impossible unless the range of issues to be settled by majority rule is severely circumscribed. In particular, government by majority rule cannot be relied upon to assign citizens' shares of the national income. *Political* assignment creates tension and conflict in society and, carried far enough, must lead to the breakdown of democracy and its replacement by another form of government.

To function, a democratic polity requires what Usher (1981: viii) refers to as a *system of equity*—"a set of rules for assigning income and other advantages independently of and prior to political decisions arrived at in the legislature." In theory, this system of equity could be based on *equality* (the assignment of equal shares), but this is "out of the question ... in a modern industrial economy because it would destroy incentives and is logically inconsistent with the minimal degree of hierarchy an industrial society requires" (Usher, 1981: 51). Rather, the only feasible system of equity is one that respects historically established property rights within the economic framework of a competitive capitalist economy. "Abolish economic freedom," concludes Usher (1981: 89), "and, regardless of one's wishes, political freedom will sooner or later be abolished as well." Only by confining democracy and respecting the system of capitalist equity can democracy be sustained.

Usher's assertion that it is necessary to restrain freedom—that is, democracy—in order to assure freedom at first appears to be either a contradiction in terms or, at best, a compromise of principles. But such is not the case, since the term freedom is used in two different senses. When Usher speaks of *political* freedom he has in mind the classical view of democracy, according to which all people have the right to be involved in making those decisions which have a significant impact on their lives and well-being. In this context, the term freedom is used in the tradition of Rousseau or Kant to mean rational self-determination (Levine, 1981: 18). But the meaning of the concept changes when *economic* freedom is discussed. Here, freedom is given the nineteenth-century liberal meaning of absence of restraint or interference (Levine, 1981: 18). To subject economic affairs to a collective, democratic process of decision making violates such freedom—in particular, the freedom to dispose of one's own property. Thus, for Usher, freedom in the first sense is only applicable to strictly "political" affairs—the choice of rulers, the passing of laws that do not concern the economy, and the like. The fact that private decisions about the disposition of property have significant effects on other individuals and on society as a whole (for example, the level of investment, the location and availability of jobs, the distribution of income entitlements) does not make them candidates for democratic decision making. The owners of property must be allowed to dispose of their resources as they see fit.

How far the state must carry this attitude of respect for the capitalist order is a matter of debate. For Usher (1981: 123), some amount of redistribution is permissible so long as it does not alter the relative positions of individuals on the scale of rich and poor. But for others (Friedman and Friedman, 1980: 93–98), programs such as the U.S. Social Security system violate the market principle because participation is obligatory (unfree) and because there is no strict correspondence between contributions and benefits. Such concepts as security, adequacy, and need are simply not market-conforming.

The conservative solution does not require the complete abandonment of the social wage. Rather, what is required is that the social-wage bill be subject to the discipline of the market and that the primacy of property rights in the wage-determination process be respected. In the area of pension policy, several proposals have been made in regard to achieving this goal.

1. *Privatization.* The most direct means of restoring market control over the "wages" of the elderly is to shift responsibility for their administration from the public to the private sector, thereby insulating these wages from the claims of citizenship. In private pension plans, benefits are calculated according to strict market principles. Social transfers on the basis of need or adequacy are nonexistent. Privatization can be achieved gradually by restricting

future growth of public sector pensions and by encouraging private saving for retirement through favorable tax laws.

2. *Limiting accessibility.* If citizenship entitlements cannot be abolished, it is possible to contain the problem by making accessibility to such entitlements more difficult. In the case of pension entitlements, this goal can be achieved by raising the age of eligibility for full benefits and by restricting or eliminating early-retirement provisions. All such efforts would result in an enlarged labor pool and, hence, greater responsiveness of market wages to fluctuations in labor demand.

3. *Make public entitlements market-conforming.* Another strategy is to administer public sector benefits according to market principles and to ensure that benefit levels and accessibility are responsive to changing market requirements. This can be achieved by eliminating the redistributive components of public pension systems, provisions for automatic indexing, allowances for dependent spouses, and other entitlements that violate market criteria.

Each of these strategies represents one means of arriving at a common objective—to impose limits on the degree to which workers in their capacity as citizens are able to claim a share of the social product over and above any claims they possess as wage-earners.

How practical is it to consider turning back the clock in this way? Goldthorpe (1978: 197) has pointed to at least three major obstacles to any such effort. The first is a cultural problem arising from the decay of the "status order"—the traditional patterns of authority and deference based on symbolic and moral definitions of social worth attached to descent, or hierarchical position. The decay of customary attitudes toward authority makes the restoration of a more "balanced" democracy (one in which economic and political elites are insulated from mass demands) exceedingly difficult. The conservative solution, therefore, first requires some form of cultural restoration of the traditional order.

The second obstacle to which Goldthorpe points is the continuing demand for more, rather than fewer, citizen entitlements. The concept of citizenship has been extended to include the workplace itself, as workers demand the right to influence the decisions that affect their terms of work and their employment opportunities. Any effort to dismantle existing entitlements will encounter considerable popular opposition, the broad support for old-age security being a case in point.

Yet a third obstacle arises from what Goldthorpe refers to as the maturation of the working class. The institutionalized power resources now available to workers enable them to oppose and resist changes that threaten their interests. The more powerful the working class, the fiercer the opposition toward conservative reforms and the more likely it is that these reforms will be achieved only if accompanied by systematic repression of working-class political and economic organizations. Goldthorpe concludes (1978: 209) that neoconservative reforms will ultimately intensify class conflict and bring "organized labor into direct confrontation with government in defense of its achieved bases of power and security." Thus, quite apart from its perceived desirability is the practicality of the neoconservative solution, which must be considered inversely proportional to the level of organizational power of the working class.

The third possibility is that the resolution of the current crisis is to be found in the proposal of Herbert Hoover's opponent in the 1928 Presidential election, Al Smith, that "the only cure for the evils of democracy is more democracy" (quoted by Huntington, 1975: 113). If democratic control over distribution is incompatible with a market-based system of production, one might conceivably restrict the latter rather than the former. The conclusion that democracy is incompatible with the capitalist accumulation process generally would suggest that democratic control should be extended to the savings and investment process and to the workplace itself. This, in essence, is the social democratic solution to the problem (Himmelstrand et al., 1981).

How would this system affect the character of old age and old-age security? It is difficult to determine the likely implications of such a solution, since there are no historical models upon which to base an analysis. In this respect, the situation of today's social democrats is analogous to that of the early philosophers of liberalism (for example, Locke and Hobbes), who struggled to convince their contemporaries of the desirability of a social order with which there was no prior experience (but see Martin, 1979). Following Usher, we might anticipate that under a system of socialist equity distribution would increasingly be based on principles of security, need, adequacy, and equality—not just for the elderly but for society as a whole. In Sweden, for example, where the social democratic experiment is quite advanced, the working-age population, as well as the old, receives a significant portion of its income through public entitlements such as family benefits. In such circumstances, the aged are less likely to be perceived as being the object of special treatment and thus as being a group apart. Since economic decisions could be based on social need rather than on profitability, work could be redesigned to accommodate an aging population, muting both the need and the desire for retirement among older workers. In sum, we might anticipate a gradual decline or at least a significant abatement of contemporary age-based criteria of social organization.

Is such a solution feasible? To many North American ears, the social democratic solution rings of romantic utopianism. But in countries where there has been more experience with democratic control of the economy, these proposals are the subject of widespread and serious debate. The re-election of the Social Democrats in Sweden in 1982, for example, promises to bring a revival and expansion of previous Swedish experiments in economic citizenship. In general, one can expect a further evolution of economic citizenship in those nations where labor is now sufficiently powerful to demand new rights over property in exchange for moderation in wage demands (see Crouch, 1979).

What is the probable outcome of such a development? The absence of historical precedent is frequently used as empirical proof that the social democratic solution is not viable. More importantly, it is argued, where the market and capitalist principles of economic organization have been abolished, dictatorship—not democracy—has followed (Geiger and Geiger, 1978: 117). This empirical demonstration, however, suffers from the fact that thus far in history socialist dictatorship has simply superseded some other form of dictatorship, as in Russia, China, and Cuba. With the short-lived exception of Chile, none of the so-called socialist societies have moved toward socialism from a democratic base, through democratic means, or, one might argue, with a democratic intent. Hence, whether it is possible to achieve a full-fledged social democracy and the total realization of citizenship that it entails is a question that can only be answered by the future.

Conclusion

If it has done nothing else, the crisis of old-age security has alerted us to the fact that the character and quality of old age in contemporary society are inextricably linked to the nature and character of the welfare state. In this chapter we have examined three possible directions in which, over the long term, this crisis of the welfare state is likely to evolve: a restoration of the rights of property and a corresponding suffocation of the rights of citizenship, a further evolution of the citizenship principle toward full economic citizenship, or a restabilization of the status quo. In the short term, however, old-age policies will reflect the halting and contradictory attempts at reform that are characteristic of all public policy formation. But this "muddling through," which seems to typify the making of social policy, should not blind us to the fact that now, as in the past, old-age policies, whether in the field of pensions, health care, or social services, are ultimately distributional policies. And in an era in which the politics of distribution have intensified (become marked by increasing conflict), it is hardly surprising that old-age policies have become the object of special attention. Like other distributional practices in the capitalist democracies, distributional policies for the elderly are a reflection of current arrangements for managing the contradictions of a democratic state in a market economy. If there is now a crisis of old-age security, it is because the existing set of arrangements for managing this relationship has been brought into question. As Marshall predicted, the principles of citizenship and social class are once again at war. The struggle over old-age security is only one of the important manifestations of this "new class war" (Piven and Cloward, 1982). It is a struggle, moreover, that will profoundly affect the future of old age. If the welfare state survives in its present form, the experience of aging in the future will be much like that of the recent past. If it is dismantled, the elderly of the future will once again experience the insecurity generated by the dynamics of the marketplace. If the citizenship principle continues to evolve, the "elderly" are likely to slowly disappear as a distinctive status group in the larger society.

Whatever the outcome, history will not come to an end; we would be presumptuous to assume that the character and experience of old age will be the same in the next century as it is in this one. In the late twentieth century, old age is retirement. And both the right to retire and the rights of the retired are the outcome of a political process. Thus, politics, not demography, determines the size of the elderly population. The social, legal, and political constituency we now call the elderly was created and given form by social, political, and economic forces; it can be destroyed or transformed by these same forces.

Notes

1. This assumption is independent of the method by which old-age pensions are financed. Whether the system is financed on a pay-as-you-go or a fully-funded basis, current consumption must ultimately be paid for out of current production—that is, by the labor of the working population.
2. Although population aging has not yet been an ostensible source of intergenerational conflict, it has produced other forms of discord and will no doubt continue to do so. These conflicts have occurred within and between sectors of the younger, more active population (professions, occupations, social institutions) that are dependent upon a particular demographic structure for their power and for their access to resources. Efforts to adapt to changing population composition have inevitably

encountered opposition because major reallocation of resources away from some sectors into others is required. Existing bases of power are eroded and new ones created. An example is the field of education. Threatened by lay-offs and lower salary increments (a result of declining enrollments), the teaching profession has responded with unionization, strikes, and an increased level of militancy in general (see Myles and Boyd, 1982).

3. Yet a fourth possibility is that from the force of the collision both principles will be destroyed and some undetermined and unpredictable social order constructed from the debris.

4. See the special issue of *The Public Interest* (1980) entitled "The Crisis in Economic Theory."

5. A more complete discussion of the rise and fall of Keynesian economic management is beyond the scope of the present work, but readers are urged to see Skidelsky (1979) for more detail.

Bibliography

Aaron, Henry
  1967 Social Security: International Comparisons. In Otto Eckstein (ed.), *Studies in Income Maintenance*, pp. 13–48. Washington, D.C.: Brookings Institution.

Achenbaum, W. Andrew
  1978 *Old Age in the New Land: The American Experience Since 1790.* Baltimore, Md.: Johns Hopkins Press.
  1980 Did Social Security Attempt to Regulate the Poor? *Research on Aging* 2 (December): pp. 470–488.
  1983 *Shades of Gray: Old Age, American Values, and Federal Policies Since 1920.* Toronto: Little, Brown and Co.

Ball, Robert
  1978 *Social Security Today and Tomorrow.* New York: Columbia University Press.

Barnes, Robert, and Sheila Zedlewski
  1981 The Impact of Inflation on the Income and Expenditures of Elderly Families. Working Paper 1401–1. Washington, D.C.: The Urban Institute.

Bell, Daniel
  1960 *The End of Ideology.* New York: Free Press.
  1976 *The Cultural Contradictions of Capitalism.* New York: Basic Books.

Bendix, Reinhard
  1956 *Work and Authority in Industry.* Berkeley: University of California Press.
  1964 *Nation-Building and Citizenship.* New York: John Wiley and Sons.

Beveridge, William Henry
  1930 *Unemployment: A Problem of Industry.* New York: Longmans, Green and Co.
  1942 *Social Insurance and Allied Services.* New York: The MacMillan Co.

1945   *Full Employment in a Free Society.* New York: W. W. Norton and Co.

Bjorn, Lars
1979   Labor Parties, Economic Growth and Redistribution in Five Capitalist Democracies. *Comparative Social Research* 2, pp. 93–128.

Block, Fred
1977   The Ruling Class Does Not Rule: Notes on the Marxist Theory of the State. *Socialist Revolution* 33 (May–June), pp. 6–27.
1981   The Fiscal Crisis of the Capitalist State. In R. Turner and J. Short (eds.), *Annual Review of Sociology* 7, pp. 1–27. Palo Alto, Cal.: Annual Reviews.

Bolger, Joe
1980   Bill C-12 and the Debate over Public Service Pension Indexing. Unpublished master's essay. Ottawa: Carleton University.

Bollen, Kenneth A.
1980   Issues in the Comparative Measurement of Political Democracy. *American Sociological Review* 80 (June), pp. 370–390.

Bowles, Samuel, and Herbert Gintis
1980   The Crisis of Liberal Democratic Capitalism. Unpublished manuscript.

Braverman, Harry
1974   *Labor and Monopoly Capital.* New York: Monthly Review Press.

Brittan, Samuel
1975   The Economic Contradictions of Democracy. *British Journal of Political Science* 5 (April), pp. 129–160.

Brown, Joan C.
1975   *How Much Choice? Retirement Policies in Canada.* Ottawa: Canadian Council on Social Development.

Bryden, Kenneth
1974   *Old Age Pensions and Policy-Making in Canada.* Montreal: McGill–Queen's University Press.

Business Committee on Pension Policy
1982   *Pension Policy—Issues and Positions. Consensus of the Business Committee on Pension Policy.* Ottawa: Business Committee on Pension Policy.

Cameron, David R.
1978   The Expansion of the Public Economy. *American Political Science Review* 72 (December), pp. 1243–1260.
1980   Economic Inequality in the Advanced Capitalist Societies: A Comparative Analysis. Paper presented at the Harvard University Centre for European Studies/Center for International Affairs on Equality and the Welfare State, Cambridge, Mass.

Canada
1979   *Retirement Age.* Ottawa: Health and Welfare Canada.

Canadian Task Force on Retirement Policy
1979   *The Retirement Income System in Canada.* Hull, Quebec: Canadian Government Publishing Centre.

Clark, Hart D.
1980   A Comparison of the Retirement Income Systems of Canada and Other Countries. Appendix 2 in *Canadian Government Task Force on*

Retirement Policy. Hull, Quebec: Canadian Government Publishing Centre.

Clark, Robert M.
1960   *Economic Security for the Aged in the United States and Canada.* Ottawa: Queen's Printer.

Clark, Robert, and David Barker
1981   *Reversing the Trend Toward Early Retirement.* Washington, D.C.: American Enterprise Institute.

Clark, Robert, and John Menefee
1981   Federal Expenditures for the Elderly: Past and Future. *The Gerontologist* 21(2), pp. 132–137.

Clark, Robert, and Joseph Spengler
1980   *The Economics of Individual and Population Aging.* Cambridge: Cambridge University Press.

Clawson, Dan
1980   *Bureaucracy and the Labour Process.* New York: Monthly Review Press.

Conrad, Christoph
1982   Aging with a Minimum of Property: The Lower Middle Class and Working Classes of Cologne, 1830–1930. Paper prepared for the annual meetings of the American Historical Association, December, 1982, Washington, D.C.

Coughlin, Richard
1979   Social Policy and Ideology: Public Opinion in Eight Rich Nations. *Comparative Social Research* 2, pp. 1–40.

Crouch, Colin
1979   The State, Capital and Liberal Democracy. In Colin Crouch (ed.), *State and Economy in Contemporary Capitalism,* pp. 13–54. London: Croom Helm.

Crozier, M., S. P. Huntington, and Joji Watanuki
1975   *The Crisis of Democracy.* Report on the Governability of Democracies to the Trilateral Commission. New York: New York University Press.

Cutwright, Phillip
1967a   Inequality: A Cross-National Analysis. *American Sociological Review* 32, pp. 562–578.
1967b   Income Redistribution: A Cross-National Analysis. *Social Forces* 46, pp. 180–190.

Davis, Kingsley, and Pietronella Van den Oever
1981   Age Relations and Public Policy in Advanced Industrial Societies. *Population and Development Review* 7 (March), pp. 1–18.

Dawson, William H.
1912   *Social Insurance in Germany, 1883–1911.* New York: Charles Scribner's Sons.

Day, Lincoln
1978   Government Pensions for the Aged in 19 Industrialized Countries. In R. Tomasson (ed.), *Comparative Studies in Sociology,* pp. 217–234. Greenwich, Conn.: JAI Press.

Derthick, Martha
  1979   *Policy-Making for Social Security.* Washington, D.C.: Brookings Institution.
Dobb, Maurice
  1946   *Studies in the Development of Capitalism.* London: Routledge and Kegan Paul.
Donahue, Wilma, Harold Orbach, and Otto Pollak
  1960   Retirement: The Emerging Social Pattern. In Clark Tibbits (ed.), *Handbook of Social Gerontology*, pp. 330–406. Chicago: University of Chicago Press.
Downs, Anthony
  1957   *An Economic Theory of Democracy.* New York: Harper and Row.
Drucker, Peter F.
  1980   Toward the Next Economics. *The Public Interest*, Special Issue, pp. 4–18.
Dye, Thomas, and L. Harmon Zeigler
  1975   *The Irony of Democracy.* North Scituate, Mass.: Duxbury Press.
Employee Benefit Research Institute
  1981   *Louis Harris Survey on the Aged.* Washington, D.C.: Employee Benefit Research Institute.
Esping-Andersen, Gösta
  1981   The Erosion of Markets and Social Policy: Power, Politics and Distribution. Paper prepared for the meetings of the European Consortium for Political Research, April, 1981, Lancaster, Great Britain.
  1982   The Welfare State as a System of Stratification. Paper presented at the Workshop on Society and Political Economy, European Consortium for Political Research, Aarhus, Denmark.
  Forthcoming   *The Social Democratic Road to Power.*
Esping-Andersen, Gösta, Roger Friedland, and Erik Wright
  1976   Modes of Class Struggle and the Capitalist State. *Kapitalstate* 4–5, pp. 186–218.
Estes, Carroll L.
  1979   *The Aging Enterprise.* San Francisco: Jossey Bass.
European Economic Community
  1977   *Social Accounts: 1970–75.* Brussels: Statistical Office of the European Communities.
Fisher, David H.
  1978   *Growing Old in America.* New York: Oxford University Press.
Flora, Peter, and Arnold Heidenheimer
  1981   The Historical Core and Changing Boundaries of the Welfare State. In Peter Flora and Arnold Heidenheimer (eds.), *The Development of Welfare States in Europe and America*, pp. 17–34. New Brunswick, N.J.: Transaction Books.
Flora, Peter, and Jens Alber
  1981   Modernization, Democratization and the Development of Welfare States in Western Europe. In Peter Flora and Arnold Heidenheimer (eds.), *The Development of Welfare States in Europe and America*, pp. 37–80. New Brunswick, N.J.: Transaction Books.

Friedman, Milton
1978   Payroll Taxes No; General Revenues Yes. In Colin Campbell (ed.),
       Financing Social Security, pp. 25–30. San Francisco: Institute for Con-
       temporary Studies.
Friedman, Milton, and Rose Friedman
1980   *Free to Choose.* New York: Avon Books.
Furniss, Norman, and Timothy Tilton
1977   *The Case for the Welfare State.* Bloomington, Ind.: Indiana University
       Press.
Gaullier, Xavier
1982   Economic Crisis and Old Age. *Aging and Society* 2 (2), pp. 165–182.
Geiger, Theodore, and Frances M. Geiger
1978   *Welfare and Efficiency. Their Interactions in Western Europe and Implications
       for International Economic Relations.* London: MacMillan.
Giddens, Anthony
1976   Classical Social Theory and the Origins of Modern Social Theory.
       American Journal of Sociology 81 (January), pp. 703–729.
Gilbert, Bentley
1966   *The Evolution of National Insurance in Great Britain: The Origins of the
       Welfare State.* London: Michael Joseph.
Goldthorpe, John
1978   The Current Inflation: Towards a Sociological Account. In Fred
       Hirsch and John Goldthorpe (eds.), *The Political Economy of Inflation*,
       pp. 186–213. Cambridge, Mass.: Harvard University Press.
Goody, Jack
1976   Aging in Nonindustrial Societies. In Robert Binstock and Ethel
       Shanas (eds.), *Handbook of Aging and the Social Sciences*, pp. 117–129.
       New York: Van Nostrand Reinhold.
Gough, Ian
1975   State Expenditures in Advanced Capitalism. *New Left Review*, 92, pp.
       53–92.
1979   *The Political Economy of the Welfare State.* London: MacMillan.
Grad, Susan, and Karen Foster
1979   Income of the Population 55 and Over, 1976. Social Security
       Administration Staff Paper No. 35. Washington, D.C.: U.S.
       Government Printing Office.
Graebner, William
1980   *A History of Retirement.* New Haven, Conn.: Yale University Press.
Gratton, Brian
1983   Social Workers and Old Age Pensions. *Social Security Review*, in
       press.
1981   Labour Force Participation Rates of Older Men, 1890–1950. Paper
       presented at the joint meeting of the Gerontological Society of
       America and the Canadian Association of Gerontology, Toronto.
Griffin, Larry, Joel Devine, and Michael Wallace
1980   Accumulation, Legitimation, and Politics: Neo-Marxist Explana-
       tions of the Growth of Welfare Expenditures in the United States
       Since the Second World War. Mimeo. Bloomington, Ind.: Indiana
       University.

Guillemard, Anne-Marie
    1980   La vieillesse et l'état. Paris: Presses Universitaires.
Gurr, Ted R.
    1978   Civil Strife Events, 1955–70. ICPSR Data Set 7531. Ann Arbor, Mich.: Inter-University Consortium for Political and Social Research.
Haanes-Olsen, Leif
    1978   Earnings-Replacement Rate of Old Age Benefits, 1965–75, Selected Countries. Social Security Bulletin (January), pp. 3–14.
Haber, Carole
    1978   Mandatory Retirement in Nineteenth-Century America: The Conceptual Basis for a New Work Cycle. Journal of Social History 12, pp. 77–96.
Hanneman, Robert
    1980   Income Inequality and Economic Development in Great Britain, Germany and France: 1850 to 1970. Comparative Social Research 3, pp. 175–184.
Headey, Bruce
    1970   Trade Unions and National Wage Policies. The Journal of Politics 32, pp. 407–439.
Heclo, Hugh
    1974   Modern Social Politics in Britain and Sweden: From Relief to Income Maintenance. New Haven, Conn.: Yale University Press.
    1981   Toward a New Welfare State? In Peter Flora and Arnold Heidenheimer (eds.), The Development of Welfare States in Europe and America, pp. 383–406. New Brunswick, N.J.: Transaction Books.
Heinz, John, and Lawton Chiles
    1981   Preface. In United States Senate Committee on Aging (ed.), Social Security in Europe: The Impact of an Aging Population, pp. iii–iv. Washington, D.C.: U.S. Government Printing Office.
Hewitt, Christopher
    1977   The Effect of Political Democracy and Social Democracy on Equality in Industrial Societies: A Cross-National Comparison. American Sociological Review 42 (June), pp. 450–464.
Hibbs, Douglas A., Jr.
    1977   Political Parties and Macroeconomic Policy. American Political Science Review 71 (December), pp. 1467–1487.
    1978   On the Political Economy of Long-Run Trends in Strike Activity. British Journal of Political Science 8 (2), pp. 153–175.
Hicks, Alexander, and Duane H. Swank
    1982   The Domestic and International Political Economy of Welfare Expansion: The Case of 17 OECD Nations, 1960–1971. Paper presented at the Annual Meeting of the American Political Science Association, St. Louis, Mo.
Himmelstrand, Ulf, Goran Ahrne, Leif Lundberg, and Lars Lundberg
    1981   Beyond Welfare Capitalism: Issues, Factors and Forces in Societal Change. London: Heinemann.
Hollingsworth, Roger, and Robert Hanneman
    1982   Leftist Governments, Working Class Power, and the Political

Economy of Advanced Capitalist Societies. In R. Tomasson (ed.), *Comparative Social Research*, Vol. 5. Greenwich, Conn.: JAI Press.

Hudson, Robert B.
1978   The "Graying" of the Federal Budget and Its Consequences for Old Age Policy. *The Gerontologist* 18 (5), pp. 428–440.

Huntington, Samuel
1975   The United States. In M. Crozier, Samuel Huntington, and Joji Watanuki (eds.), *The Crisis of Democracy*, pp. 59–118. New York: New York University Press.

International Labour Organization
Various years   *The Cost of Social Security*. Geneva, Switzerland: ILO.

Jackman, Robert
1975   *Politics and Social Equality: A Comparative Analysis*. New York: John Wiley and Sons.

Jensen, Carsten V.
1981   *Danish Pension Policy. Elements to a Study of the Dual Welfare State*. Roskilde, Denmark: Institute of Economics and Planning.

Kaim-Caudle, P. R.
1973   *Comparative Social Policy and Social Security: A Ten Country Study*. London: Martin Robertson and Co.

Kerr, Clark, J. T. Dunlop, Frederick Harbison, and Charles Myers
1964   *Industrialism and Industrial Man*. New York: Oxford University Press.

Key, V. O.
1949   *Southern Politics*. New York: Alfred Knopf and Sons.

Keyfitz, Nathan
1980   Why Social Security Is in Trouble. *The Public Interest* 58, pp. 102–119.

Kohl, Jurgen
1981   Trends and Problems in Post-War Public Expenditure Development in Western Europe and America. In Peter Flora and Arnold Heidenheimer (eds.), *The Development of the Welfare State in Europe and America*, pp. 307–344. New Brunswick, N.J.: Transaction Books.

Korpi, Walter
1980   Social Policy and Distributional Conflict in the Capitalist Democracies. A Preliminary Comparative Framework. *West European Politics* 3 (October), pp. 296–315.

Korpi, Walter, and Michael Shalev
1979   Strikes, Industrial Relations and Class Conflict in Capitalist Societies. *British Journal of Sociology* 30 (2), 164–187.
1980   Strikes, Power and Politics in the Western Nations, 1900–1976. In Maurice Zeitlin (ed.), *Political Power and Social Theory*, Vol. I, pp. 301–334. Greenwich, Conn.: JAI Press.

Kreps, Juanita
1976   The Economy and the Aged. In Robert Binstock and Ethel Shanas (eds.), *Handbook of Aging and the Social Sciences*, pp. 272–285. New York: Van Nostrand Reinhold.

Laffer, Arthur, and David Ranson
1977   A Proposal for Reforming Social Security. In G. S. Tolley and

Richard V. Burkhauser (eds.), *Income Support for the Aged*, pp. 133–150. Cambridge, Mass.: Ballinger.

Laslett, Peter
1976   Societal Development and Aging. In Robert Binstock and Ethel Shanas (eds.), *Handbook of Aging and the Social Sciences*, pp. 87–96. New York: Van Nostrand Reinhold.

Leimer, Dean
1979   Projected Rates of Return to Future Social Security Retirees Under Alternative Benefit Structures. In *Social Security Administration Policy Analysis with Social Security Files*, Research Report No. 52, pp. 235–257. Washington, D.C.: U.S. Government Printing Office.

Lenski, Gerhard
1966   *Power and Privilege*. Toronto: McGraw-Hill.

Levine, Andrew
1981   *Liberal Democracy. A Critique of Its Theory*. New York: Columbia University Press.

Lindblom, Charles
1977   *Politics and Markets*. New York: Basic Books.

Lipset, Seymour Martin
1960   *Political Man*. Garden City, N.Y.: Doubleday.

Lubove, R.
1968   *The Struggle for Social Security, 1900–1935*. Cambrige, Mass.: Harvard University Press.

Mackie, Thomas, and Richard Rose
1974   International Almanac of Election Statistics. London: MacMillan.

Maguire, Maria
1981   Pension Policy: An Overview of Patterns of Development and the Impact of Party. Paper presented at the meetings of European Consortium for Political Research, April, 1981, Lancaster, Great Britain.

Marshall, T. H.
1964   *Class, Citizenship, and Social Development*. Chicago: University of Chicago Press.

Martin, Andrew
1973   *The Politics of Economic Policy in the United States: A Tentative View from a Comparative Perspective*. Beverly Hills, Cal.: Sage Publications.
1975   Is Democratic Control of Capitalist Economies Possible? In Leon Lindberg et al. (eds.), *Stress and Contradiction in Modern Capitalism*. Lexington, Mass.: D. C. Heath.
1979   The Dynamics of Change in a Keynesian Political Economy: The Swedish Case and Its Implications. In Colin Crouch (ed.), *State and Economy in Contemporary Capitalism*, pp. 88–121. London: Croom Helm.

McDonald, Linda, and E. Bower Carty
1979   Effect of Projected Population Change on Expenditures of Government. Appendix 16 in *Canadian Government Task Force on Retirement Policy*. Hull, Quebec: Canadian Govenment Publishing Centre.

Melchers, R. F.
1980   Action sociale patronale et rapports de production: les origines des régimes de retraites d'entreprise au Canada, 1870–1914. Aix-en-Provence, France: Centre National de la Recherche Scientifique.

Miliband, Ralph
1969   *The State in Capitalist Society.* London: Weidenfeld and Nicholson.

Mills, C. Wright
1951   *White Collar.* New York: Oxford University Press.
1959   *The Sociological Imagination.* New York: Oxford University Press.

Munnell, Alicia
1981   Social Security, Private Pensions and Saving. Paper prepared for the Conference on Public Policy Issues in the Financing of Retirement, January 16–17, 1981, Alexandria, Va.

Murphy, Barbara
1982   Corporate Capital and the Welfare State: Canadian Business and Public Pension Policy in Canada Since World War II. Unpublished master's thesis. Ottawa: Carleton University.

Myles, John F.
1980   The Aged, the State and the Structure of Inequality. In J. Harp and J. Hofley (eds.), *Structured Social Inequality.* Toronto: Prentice-Hall.
1981   The Trillion Dollar Misunderstanding: Social Security's Real Crisis. *Working Papers Magazine* 8 (4), pp. 22–31.

Myles, John, and Monica Boyd
1982   Population Aging and the Elderly. In D. Forcese and S. Richer (eds.), *Social Issues. Sociological Views of Canada*, pp. 258–285. Scarborough, Ontario: Prentice-Hall.

Notestein, Frank, et al.
1944   *The Future Population of Europe and the Soviet Union, Population Projections 1940–1970.* Geneva, Switzerland: League of Nations.

O'Connor, James
1970   Some Contradictions of Advanced U.S. Capitalism. *Social Theory and Practice* 1, pp. 1–11.
1973   *The Fiscal Crisis of the State.* New York: St. Martin's Press.

Offe, Claus
1972   Advanced Capitalism and the Welfare State. *Politics and Society* 2, pp. 479–488.

Organization for Economic Cooperation and Development
1976   *Public Expenditure on Income Maintenance Programs.* Paris: OECD.
1977   *Old Age Pension Schemes.* Paris: OECD.
1979   *Socioeconomic Policies for the Elderly.* Paris: OECD.

Pampel, Fred, and Jane Weiss
1983   Economic Development, Pension Policies, and the Labor Force Participation of Aged Males: A Cross-National, Longitudinal Study. *American Journal of Sociology* 89 (Sept): 350–372.

Parkin, Frank
1972   *Class Inequality and Political Order.* New York: Praeger Publishers.

Parsons, Talcott
1971   *The System of Modern Societies.* Englewood Cliffs, N.J.: Prentice-Hall.

Pentland, H. Clare
1981   *Labour and Capital in Canada 1650–1860*. Toronto: James Lorimer and Co.
Perrin, Guy
1969   Reflections on Fifty Years of Social Security. *International Labour Review* 99 (3), pp. 249–290.
Pesando, James, and S. A. Rea
1977   *Public and Private Pensions in Canada: An Economic Analysis*. Toronto: University of Toronto Press.
Piven, Frances F., and Richard A. Cloward
1971   *Regulating the Poor: The Functions of Public Welfare*. New York: Vintage Books.
1982   *The New Class War*. New York: Pantheon Books.
Polanyi, Karl
1944   *The Great Transformation*. Boston: Beacon Press.
Pollard, Sydney
1964   *The Genesis of Modern Management: A Study of the Industrial Revolution in Great Britain*. Cambridge, Mass.: Harvard University Press.
Pryor, Frederic L.
1968   *Public Expenditures in Communist and Capitalist Nations*. Homewood, Ill.: Irwin.
1973   *Property and Industrial Organization in Communist and Capitalist Countries*. Bloomington, Ind.: Indiana University Press.
Rimlinger, Gaston
1971   *Welfare Policy and Industrialization in Europe, America and Russia*. Toronto: John Wiley and Sons.
Rosa, Jean-Jacques (ed.)
1982   *The World Crisis in Social Security*. San Francisco: Institute for Contemporary Studies.
Ross, Stanford G.
1979   Social Security: A World-Wide Issue. *Social Security Bulletin* 42 (8), pp. 3–10.
Rothman, David
1971   *The Discovery of the Asylum*. Boston: Little, Brown and Co.
Rubinow, I. M.
1911   *Social Insurance: With Special Reference to American Conditions*. New York: Henry Holt.
Rubinson, Richard
1977   Reply to Bach and Irwin. *American Sociological Review* 42 (5), pp. 817–821.
Sauvy, Alfred
1948   Social and Economic Consequences of the Aging of Western European Populations. *Population Studies* 2 (1), pp. 115–124.
Schottland, Charles I.
1967   *The Welfare State. Selected Essays*. New York: Harper and Row.
Schulz, James
1980   *The Economics of Aging*. Belmont, Cal.: Wadsworth.

Schulz, James, Guy Carrin, Hans Krupp, Manfred Peschke, Elliot Sclar, and J. Van Steenberge
  1974   *Providing Adequate Retirement Income—Pension Reform in the United States and Abroad.* Hanover, N.H.: Brandeis University Press.
Schumpeter, Joseph
  1950   *Capitalism, Socialism and Democracy.* New York: Harper Bros.
Simmons, Leo
  1960   Aging in Preindustrial Societies. In Clark Tibbitts (ed.), *Handbook of Social Gerontology*, pp. 62–91. Chicago: University of Chicago Press.
Skidelsky, Robert
  1979   The Decline of Keynesian Politics. In Colin Crouch (ed.), *State and Economy in Contemporary Capitalism*, pp. 55–87. London: Croom Helm.
Skocpol, Theda, and John Ikenberry
  1982   The Political Formation of the American Welfare State. Paper presented at the Annual Meeting of the American Sociological Association, September, 1982, San Francisco.
Splane, R. B.
  1965   *Social Welfare in Ontario, 1791–1883: A Study of Public Welfare Administration.* Toronto: University of Toronto Press.
Stack, J.
  1978   Internal Political Organization and the World Economy of Income Inequality. *American Sociological Review* 43, pp. 271–272.
Stearns, Peter
  1976   *Old Age in Industrial Society: The Case of France.* New York: Holmes and Meiers.
Stephens, John
  1979   *The Transition from Capitalism to Socialism.* London: MacMillan.
Swank, Duane
  1981   Between Revolution and Incrementalism. Paper presented at the meetings of the American Sociological Association, Toronto.
Therborn, Goran
  1977   The Rule of Capital and the Rise of Democracy. *New Left Review* 103 (May–June), pp. 3–41.
Tomasson, Richard F.
  1982   Government Old Age Pensions Under Affluence and Austerity: West Germany, Sweden, the Netherlands, and the United States. Paper presented at the meetings of the Tenth World Congress of the International Sociological Association, August, 1982, Mexico City.
Torrey, Barbara, and Carole Thompson
  1980   *An International Comparison of Pension Systems.* Washington, D.C.: President's Commission on Pension Policy.
Tufte, Edward R.
  1978   *Political Control of the Economy.* Princeton, N.J.: Princeton University Press.

Union of Swiss Banks
   1977   *Social Security in 10 Industrial Nations.* Zurich, Switzerland: Union Bank of Switzerland.
United Nations
   1956   *The Aging of Populations and Its Economic and Social Implication.* New York: United Nations.
   1976   *Statistical Yearbook.* New York: United Nations.
United States Department of Health and Human Services
   1980   *Private Pension Plans in West Germany and France.* Social Security Administration Research Report No. 5. Washington, D.C.: U.S. Government Printing Office.
United States Senate Committee on Aging
   1981   *Social Security in Europe: The Impact of an Aging Population.* Washington, D.C.: U.S. Government Printing Office.
Usher, Dan
   1981   *The Economic Prerequisite to Democracy.* Oxford: Basil Blackwell.
Wander, Hilde
   1978   ZPG Now: The Lesson from Europe. In Thomas Espenshade and William Serow (eds.)., *The Economic Consequences of Slowing Population Growth*, pp. 41–69. New York: Academic Press.
Weede, Erich
   1980   Sociological Analyses of Income Inequality. *American Sociological Review* 45 (June), pp. 497–501.
Wilensky, Harold
   1975   *The Welfare State and Equality.* Berkeley: University of California Press.
   1976   *The "New Corporatism," Centralization, and the Welfare State.* Beverly Hills, Cal.: Sage.
   1981   Leftism, Catholicism and Democratic Corporatism: The Role of Political Parties in Recent Welfare State Development. In Peter Flora and Arnold Heidenheimer (eds.), *The Development of Welfare States in Europe and America*, pp. 345–382. New Brunswick, N.J.: Transaction Books.
Wilson, Thomas (ed.)
   1974   *Pensions, Inflation and Growth.* London: Heinemann.
Wolfe, Alan
   1977   *The Limits of Legitimacy.* New York: Free Press.

Index

135